LECH WALESA
AND
POLAND

LECH WALESA AND POLAND

DENNIS VNENCHAK

An Impact Biography
FRANKLIN WATTS
NEW YORK • CHICAGO • LONDON • TORONTO • SYDNEY

Photographs copyright ©: AP/Wide World Photos: pp. 1, 2 bottom, 6 bottom, 8, 11, 12 top, 13, 14, 16; UPI/Bettmann Newsphotos: pp. 2 top, 3, 4, 5, 6 top, 7, 9, 10; Reuters/Bettmann Newsphotos: pp. 12 bottom, 15 bottom; Impact Visuals/Larry Boyd: p. 15 top.

Library of Congress Cataloging-in-Publication Data

Vnenchak, Dennis.
Lech Walesa and Poland/Dennis Vnenchak.
p. cm.
An Impact biography
Includes bibliographical references and index.
Summary: Examines Poland's history, with particular emphasis on the role of Lech Walesa, the former labor leader who was elected president in 1990.
ISBN 0-531-11128-8
1. Walesa, Lech, 1943– —Juvenile literature. 2. Presidents—Poland—Biography—Juvenile literature. 3. Poland—History—Juvenile literature. [1. Walesa, Lech, 1943– . 2. Presidents—Poland. 3. Poland—History. 4. Labor unions—Biography.]
I. Title.
DK4452.W34V59 1994
943.805′6′092—dc20
[B] 92-40266
CIP AC

Printed in the United States of America
5 4 3 2 1

CONTENTS

INTRODUCTION

On the night of August 15, 1980, Lech Walesa (pronounced Lehk Vah-whén-sah), a worker at a Gdansk shipyard who had been fired from his job for his political activism, jumped over the fence of the shipyard to join his fellow workers in their strike to protest the government's newly announced price hikes. In doing so, he was to change Polish history in a way that would also have far-reaching consequences for the rest of the world.

The story of Lech Walesa's Poland is the story of a struggle for freedom. In fact, all of Poland's history can be summed up in the phrase "struggle for freedom." Poland's existence as an independent state has often been in jeopardy. The political history of Poland has been a story of how Poles have tried to defend their country against the loss of independence or, more frequently, the story of their attempts to get it back. The struggle for political freedom has taken many different forms and has manifested itself in many ways. For example, from the late eighteenth century to the end of World War I, Poland did not exist as an independent nation. It disappeared from the map of Europe in 1795, when it was completely divided up, or partitioned, by Russia, Prussia, and Austria. Throughout this period of approximately 125 years, the Poles did not lose their "Polishness" (*polskość*). Instead, they dreamed of getting their freedom back and establishing a truly independent nation, a sovereign (or self-governing) state they could call their own.

This spirit of nationalism, while deeply affecting all of Europe, was particularly strong in Poland. At the end of World War I, the dream of an independent Poland seemed to come true; Poland was reborn as a sovereign state in 1918. But the dream was cut short on September 1, 1939, when Hitler's forces invaded Poland and took its freedom away once again. As part of a pact with Nazi Germany, the Soviet Union invaded sixteen days later and occupied Poland's eastern territories. It seemed as if another in a long series of partitions by Germany and Russia had begun. Once again Poland's freedom was lost. Poles shed their blood in an effort to regain it; but even the defeat of Hitler in World War II did not bring to fulfillment the dream of independence. Poland remained a subjugated nation, a so-called satellite state of the Soviet Union. Poland became one of the countries of East Central Europe that was forced into communism by Joseph Stalin, the ruthless dictator of the Soviet Union.

The story of Lech Walesa is really a continuation of this theme of Polish history. The struggle for freedom he took part in was against a foreign political and economic system imposed on Poles by the Communist party leadership of the Soviet Union in the aftermath of World War II. Lech Walesa is sometimes portrayed as the man who "brought down Communism" in East Central Europe. Although this is an exaggeration, there is little doubt that he played a crucial role in the achievement of this end. An electrician by trade, Walesa became the leader of the so-called strike for freedom at the Gdansk shipyard in August 1980. This strike led to the creation of a free and independent trade union called Solidarity. It was the first time that a trade union free of Communist party control had been allowed to exist in the Soviet bloc.

Walesa's success shocked not only the Communist world but the Western world as well. The rise of the Solidarity trade union in Poland in 1980 ushered in the most broadly based challenge to Communist rule the world had yet seen. Was the

Communist party, supposedly the representative of the working people, willing to share its power with an independent workers' union led by Lech Walesa? Would the Communist party leaders of Poland permit this development to take place? What would it mean for the continuation of their own power? Would the Soviet Union allow it to continue? And more important, would it spread to other countries of East Central Europe and possibly even to the Soviet Union itself? These were some of the questions for which the world awaited answers at that time.

Lech Walesa has an impressive list of accomplishments qualifying him as a worthy subject for historical investigation. In the summer of 1980 he became one of the most famous men in the world. The creation of the Solidarity trade union in 1980 was only the beginning. In January 1982 Walesa was named *Time* magazine's man of the year for 1981, and in 1983 he was awarded the Nobel Peace Prize for his efforts to achieve a nonviolent, democratic solution to the Polish problem. But his greatest accomplishment may have occurred in 1989, when he showed himself to be a shrewd and cunning political strategist. He helped engineer the compromise which, for the first time in history, placed a non-Communist government at the head of a Soviet satellite state. By 1990 this same man was running for president of Poland in free and democratic elections.

The Communist party of Poland was suddenly absent from the political arena. It had declined rapidly, and Solidarity easily occupied the political vacuum that had been created. Lech Walesa, the leader of an independent trade union, became president of the country on December 12, 1990. More important, however (and Walesa would be the first to agree), Poland had at last achieved real political independence. Forty-five years of Soviet-sponsored Communist rule had come to an end. Poland's freedom had been won, in large measure because of the efforts of an electrician from the Lenin shipyards in Gdansk. More than any other single Pole, Lech Walesa had made it happen.

LITHUANIA
RUSSIA
BALTIC SEA
RUSSIA
BELARUS
Gdynia
Gdańsk
Szczecin
Bydgoszcz
Berlin
Poznań
Warsaw
POLAND
GERMANY
Radom
Lublin
Bonn
Wrocław
UKRAINE
Katowice
Prague
Craców
CZECH
REPUBLIC
SLOVAKIA
Bratislava
Vienna
Budapest
AUSTRIA
ROMANIA
HUNGARY
BLACK
SEA

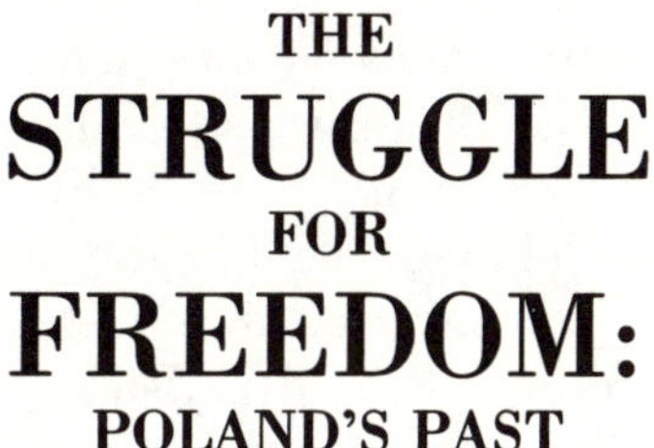

THE STRUGGLE FOR FREEDOM: POLAND'S PAST

The history of the Polish struggle
is often a struggle for Polish history.[1]

LAWRENCE WESCHLER

Lech Walesa is a Pole, and he speaks the Polish language. Polish belongs to the Slavic language group and therefore is similar to the languages of the Russians, Czechs, Slovaks, Ukrainians, and Bulgarians. Poland as a country is approximately the same size as New Mexico. While Poland has often been referred to as a part of Eastern Europe, Poland lies at the center of the European continent. However, many political analysts ignored the vast expanse of territory between Poland and the Ural Mountains, which was still technically a part of Europe. They preferred to see Poland and some of its neighbors as lying at the doorstep of the former Soviet Union, a giant superpower whose vast territories extended well into Asia. In some sense, Europe was seen as ending where the Soviet Union began. Although this outlook was geographically incorrect, it did make some sense politically to refer to Poland as a part of Eastern Europe, and it is in this sense only that the use of the term was appropriate. The use of the term Central Europe was often reserved for such countries as Germany, Austria, and Switzerland. The Soviet bloc countries as a whole were generally described as belonging to Eastern Europe.

Proper terminology with regard to Poland's location in Europe has become more important in the post–Cold War period. With the breakup of the Soviet Union in 1991 and the institution of separate statehood for such former Soviet republics as Ukraine and Byelorussia (Belarus), it is no longer appropriate to use the term "Eastern Europe" to refer to Poland. A possible solution is to use the term "East Central Europe" to refer to Poland's location.

From earliest times, Poland's history has been conditioned largely by its geographical location in the center of Europe. Lying between Germanic-speaking peoples to the west and Russians to the east, for most of its history Poland has had to deal with these two strong neighbors, both of whom at various times have had designs on Polish territories. In its early history Poland, too, occasionally played the role of aggressor and dominated some of its neighbors. But geography has created for Poland some unique and very powerful obstacles to the preservation of its own independence. Most of Poland is flat and easily accessible to foreign invaders. Except for the impressive Tatra Mountains to the south, no real natural boundaries clearly define Poland's borders. Crossing a river on a flat plain was about all a potential invader had to contend with, a fact that Poland's neighbors all too frequently took advantage of. The struggle to defend the sanctity of its borders against foreign invasion has long been part of the Polish experience.

EARLY HISTORY

The recorded history of Poland dates back to the tenth century A.D. Before that time, the territory we now know as

Poland was inhabited by various Slavic-speaking tribes. Most famous among them were the Polanie, or Polanians, from whom Poland got its name. By the ninth century these tribes had begun to develop more complex political organizations. The stronger tribes conquered the weaker, and in this way various primitive states were formed. The Polanie built the strongest of these emerging state organizations, and by the tenth century they had succeeded in uniting most of the Polish-speaking lands under their rule.

The emergence of state organizations was a common political trend in East Central Europe at that time. Poland saw its neighbors—Bohemia, the land of the present-day Czechs; Hungary; and Rus, Russian territories—undergo the same political changes. To the west, the Germanic tribes had gone through the process slightly earlier. Each of these emerging state organizations had a powerful military force that had to be taken seriously. Each was a threat to the very existence of the others, and warfare among them was quite common.

The first historical ruler of Poland was Mieszko I of the Piast dynasty. He married a Bohemian princess and in the year 966 adopted Christianity. The entire Polish nation soon adopted the new religion of its ruler. This event had profound consequences on the entire development of Polish history, and Poland's deep religious faith can be seen to the present day. Significantly, the conversion to Christianity brought Poland into the sphere of Western civilization and culture. Poland was the most easterly land in Europe to be brought directly into Western civilization. Lands farther to the east, including Russia and Ukraine, were also brought into Christianity, but they adopted the Eastern Orthodox faith and were more affected by that cultural experience. As a result, while Russia remained largely outside the Western cultural experience, Poland was drawn into it.

In 1386 a new period of Polish history began with the marriage of Queen Jadwiga of Poland and Ladislaus Jagiello, grand duke of Lithuania. This marriage marked the beginning of the Jagiellonian dynasty, which was to rule Poland until 1572. The union of Jadwiga and Jagiello was not simply a marriage of two individuals; it was a personal union with profound political implications. It joined the two lands into a single Polish-Lithuanian kingdom. (Legal formation of a new Polish-Lithuanian commonwealth, however, did not come until the Union of Lublin in 1569.) Poland became much stronger militarily and, as a result, was better able to defeat its political enemies. The most menacing enemy was the Teutonic Order of the German Knights. These knights had settled on Polish territory at the invitation of a Polish king in the twelfth century but gradually began to threaten Polish rule. In 1410 Polish and Lithuanian forces defeated the Teutonic Order at the battle of Grünwald, known in Germany as the battle of Tannenberg. The victory was important because it ensured Poland's political independence from the Germans. Today it is still widely celebrated in Poland as a symbol of successful resistance to the German threat.

The next centuries saw an expansion of Polish culture as well as Polish territories. Poland became the largest state in Europe. The sixteenth century became known as the golden age of Poland. It was the time of the Polish Renaissance, which included the development of a literary native language as well as a flowering of education, political and legal thought, the arts, and architecture. It was also the period of great scientific discoveries, including those of Nicolaus Copernicus, a Polish astronomer whose work served to revolutionize people's view of our place in the solar system.

When the last of the Jagiellonian kings died without an heir in 1572, Poland entered a new period of elective monarchy. The succession of kings was no longer based on heredity. Instead of the usual pattern of the king's son becoming the new king upon his father's death, Polish kings were now selected by special assemblies of the Polish nobility. An unusual historical pattern was thus created in which kings were elected by a process of voting. This period of Polish history lasted until 1795, when Poland ceased to exist as an independent European state.

The period from 1572 to 1795 is sometimes referred to as the Commonwealth of the Gentry (in Polish, *szlachta,* the nobility, the aristocracy). The nobility of Poland, especially the so-called magnates—the wealthiest nobles who owned huge tracts of land—became quite strong and independent. Any contender for the Polish throne had to make considerable concessions to secure the magnates' votes. The magnates did not want the king to interfere in their local affairs, and they preserved their own local power by refusing to let the Polish kings become too strong. The Polish nobility was thus relatively free from any domination by the monarch and was experiencing what it liked to call its "golden freedom."

While Western Europe, especially France, was going through its Age of Absolutism, in which the monarchs centralized and strengthened their power, in Poland the nobility was jealously guarding its own freedom against any meddling by the Polish king. Although this concern for freedom may seem admirable, the nobles were actually trying to protect their own interests. From the standpoint of Poland's neighbors, the end result was the development of a weak nation ruled by a weak and largely ineffective Polish monarch.

The symbol of this excessive freedom for the nobility was a rule called the *liberum veto*. This rule allowed a single deputy at a meeting of Poland's parliament (called the Sejm) to reject or veto any proposal he did not like. From the seventeenth century on, this rule increasingly had been used to block the legislative proposals of political opponents. Foreign powers in particular found this an effective way to intervene in Polish affairs; they could successfully block any reform measure they did not like if they could persuade even a single Polish deputy to cast a negative vote. The increased abuse of this rule hindered any attempt at reforming the system, or making any changes at all, since someone could always be found to object and cast a veto.

Very often the nobles would offer the Polish throne to a foreigner rather than let a Polish king become too powerful. During this period, French, German, and Swedish monarchs ruled Poland; they did not always have Poland's best interests at heart. Foreign kings also brought with them increased foreign intervention in Poland's external affairs. One result was that Poland was unnecessarily involved in many wars, including wars with Russians, Turks, Tatars, and Swedes. A war with Sweden deserves particular mention. Polish kings from 1587 to 1668 were Catholic Swedes of the Vasa dynasty who refused to give up their dynastic claims to Protestant Sweden. They wanted to rule over Poland and Sweden at the same time. This dispute eventually led to war. In 1655 Swedish armies attacked Poland; nearly every part of the country was occupied by Swedish armies at one time or another during the war. Over a period of five years the entire country was devastated. A famous Polish writer, Henryk Sienkiewicz, described the entire affair in his book *Potop* (*The Deluge*). The war with Sweden was just one more contributing factor that led to a general decline in the country as a whole.

The war with Sweden also illustrated the identification of religion with the struggle for Polish national freedom. Religious beliefs of the Catholic church were closely linked to the fight against the foreign invader. Swedish armies had traversed the Polish countryside almost at will, wreaking tremendous havoc. By 1656 only one major Polish city was still holding out, namely the town of Czestochowa, the site of Jasna Gora, or the Mountain of Light, Poland's most sacred monastery. Despite a huge effort on the part of the Swedish army, the heavily fortified monastery held off the Swedish advance. Sienkiewicz described the scene this way:

> Soon smoke and the odor of burning filled all the interior of buildings. . . . The heaviest bombs burst even through ceilings. . . . Windows were bursting from heat, and women and children confined in rooms were stifling from smoke and exhalations. Hardly were some missiles extinguished . . . when there came new flocks of burning balls, flaming clothes, sparks, living fire. The whole cloister was seized with it. . . . Still it burned, but was not consumed; it was flaming, but did not fall to fragments. . . . The besieged began to sing like those youths

> in the fiery furnace. . . . To the men standing at the walls and working at the guns . . . that song was like healing balsam, announcing continually that the church was standing, that the cloister was standing, that so far flames had not vanquished the efforts of men.[2]

The battle of Jasna Gora marked the beginning of the turnaround by which Poland was able to regain its conquered territories. The people in the monastery of Czestochowa attributed their success to the direct intervention of the Virgin Mary. Miraculously, despite the fact that nearly everything in the monastery was burned, the painting of the Virgin holding the baby Jesus had managed to survive intact. This painting, known as the Black Madonna, became an instant symbol of the struggle of the Polish nation against foreign aggression. It was a symbol that would be remembered well by Lech Walesa in his own struggle for freedom in 1980.

From the very beginning, religion in Poland was intertwined with national identity. Since Christianity was introduced into Poland in 966, Poland has remained a strong bastion for the church. Even during the turbulent period in European history known as the Protestant Reformation, Poland's faith in the Catholic church remained strong. While other countries were torn by bloody religious wars, Poland was able to avoid serious religious confrontation. Substantial religious toleration in Poland provided a sharp contrast to the bloody wars of religion in Western Europe. Poland even became a safe haven for persecuted religious groups. For example, it was during this period that many Jews immigrated to Poland to escape, at least for a time, the religious persecution they experienced elsewhere in Europe.

Catholicism became closely associated with Polish national identity. In the minds of most Poles, "to be Polish" and "to be Catholic" went hand in hand. Thus there could never be any real contradiction between being a good Pole and being a good Catholic. What helped establish this close association of religion and national identity was the interplay of geography, politics, and religion. Poland's most powerful neighbors, and thus potential political enemies, were nations whose religion was not Roman Catholic. To the east were the Russians, whose religion stemmed from the Greek Orthodox sect of Christianity. To the west were the Germans, who belonged largely to Protestant sects, especially Lutheranism. The Scandinavian countries to the north were also largely Protestant. And to the south, Bohemia was largely occupied by the Protestant Czechs. The Polish Catholics were thus surrounded by often hostile neighbors of different religious persuasions. Protecting the nation came to mean defending the faith itself.

THE PARTITION PERIOD

The political and economic decline of Poland continued through the next century. General political weakness in the country continued at a time when Poland's neighbors were becoming more and more powerful. Prussia, Austria, and Russia had become first-rate military powers, and these emerging states used Poland's weakness for their own political gain. In the late eighteenth century, these three powers formed a triple alliance against Poland. They jointly decided to carve up Polish territory and divide the spoils among themselves. In three successive partitions—1772, 1793, and 1795—Poland's territory was gradually reduced until the country known as Poland no longer existed.

The three partitioning powers offered no excuse for their annexation of Polish territories other than a vague desire "to secure the stability of Europe." But they had no valid reasons to justify their actions. They simply did it because they were powerful enough to get away with it. Foreign intervention in Polish affairs had long caused much trouble for Poland. Now it had caused the Polish state to cease to exist altogether, and its territories were incorporated into the borders of the three partitioning powers.

The tragic aspect of this period in Polish history is that the partitions came at a time when Poland was finally embarking on a period of major reform. If this reform had been achieved, Poland might have been saved from the abyss it had moved toward. In the second half of the eighteenth century Poland was influenced by the ideas of the Enlightenment, a period in Western history that emphasized the use of reason and observation to improve human social institutions. There was much talk of political reform based on the application of Enlightenment principles. In 1773, for example, the world's first ministry of education, the Commission of National Education, was founded in Poland.

But it was the Polish constitution of May 3, 1791, that represented the culmination of the reform movement. It was modeled to some extent on the American Constitution, which had also been influenced by Enlightenment ideas, and it offered many of the same freedoms. According to the May constitution, sovereignty in Poland would be based upon the law, with guarantees of individual liberty. This document would have made Poland a constitutional monarchy. Among other things, it proposed the elimination of the *liberum veto* rule, which had so hampered Poland's development. The May 1791 constitution was Europe's first (slightly before the French constitution of the same year) and the world's second (after the American) written constitution.[3]

Unfortunately, the reforms promised in the Polish constitution of 1791 were short-lived. Not all of Polish society was committed to reform. Certain conservative, or reactionary, elements of Polish nobility, mostly among the magnates, were strongly opposed to any changes that might undermine their power. They organized the Confederation of Targowica in an attempt to overthrow the new constitution, and they actually invited foreign aid in eliminating the reforms. Poland was on the verge of civil war over this issue when foreign powers stepped in and ended the dispute in favor of the reactionaries. The constitution was quickly abolished by the partitioning powers. In the process, more Polish lands were lost in the second partition of Poland.

The Poles refused to accept the loss of their independence without a fight. After the second partition of Poland in

1793, a major revolt to try to regain the lost Polish territories took place. Tadeusz Kosciuszko, a Polish general who had helped Washington fight for America's independence from Great Britain in 1776, led the Polish insurrection. It was a popular uprising that involved the participation of thousands of peasants rather than the traditional military. Although General Kosciuszko and his peasant soldiers fought valiantly, their attempt to restore Poland's independence was unsuccessful. The combined forces of the triple alliance were too powerful. Kosciuszko was wounded in battle and was captured by the opposition forces. Nevertheless, he immediately became a national hero to the Poles and, from that moment on, served as a national symbol of the struggle for Poland's freedom. The failure of the Kosciuszko insurrection brought down the full wrath of the foreign powers on Poland. In 1795 they completed their third partition, and Poland completely disappeared from the map of Europe.

During the course of the next century, Poles tried repeatedly to regain their lost independence and reestablish Poland as a nation. Their efforts were unsuccessful. A near success did come shortly after the turn of the nineteenth century, when French armies under Napoleon were fighting Russia, Prussia, and Austria. France became the natural ally of the Poles. It was during this time that the following words were written: "Poland has not yet perished as long as we are alive. What a foreign power has taken away from us, we will regain with our swords."

These words later became the opening lines of the Polish national anthem. They vividly illustrate the historical willingness of Poles to fight for their political freedom. Written to the tune of a mazurka (a Polish folk dance) in 1797 by Józef Wybicki, this song soon became a rallying cry for Polish soldiers in Italy under the command of General Jan Dabrowski. The Polish legions in Italy were fighting alongside the French army of Napoleon against the Germans, Austrians, and Russians in the belief that Napoleon would help restore Poland's independence. One writer described the situation this way: "The song of the Legions became the symbol of

Poland's indestructibility and faith in her rebirth, a symbol rallying all Poles, with no distinction as to social rank, in the struggle for the nation's freedom. It was sung on the particularly solemn and historic occasions. It resounded on the fields of insurrectionary battles and in street demonstrations."[4]

Napoleon appeared to offer the Poles a chance to regain their lost independence, and many Poles placed a great deal of hope and trust in his promise. For a time he seemed partially to keep his word by aiding in the formation of the so-called Grand Duchy of Warsaw, a resurrected portion of the Polish state. But with Napoleon's defeat, all Polish hopes of independence were shattered, and the Duchy of Warsaw collapsed. At the Congress of Vienna in 1815, a new division of Polish territories among Russia, Prussia, and Austria was affirmed. Some historians speak of this event as the "fourth partition of Poland." (A fifth partition was yet to come in 1939, when Hitler's Germany and Stalin's Russia were to divide Polish lands once again.) But the words the Polish legions sang were not forgotten. The sentence "Poland has not yet perished as long as we are alive" was translated into various languages and became a declaration in favor of the freedom of all nations. During World War II it was sung in obvious reference to the Nazi occupation of Poland. And Lech Walesa and the other striking workers of Gdansk would also sing it in 1980.

Before the end of the nineteenth century, however, Poles made at least two more serious attempts at restoring Poland's status as an independent nation. In the Polish uprisings of November 1830 and January 1863 against the domination of Russia, the Dabrowski mazurka was sung once again in the nationalist cause of Polish independence. Poland's freedom had been threatened so many times in the past that this tune seemed the obvious choice. But these uprisings ended in tragic failure; the Poles were no match for the armies of the Russian czars. The punishment for starting these revolts was the introduction of even more repressive political measures. One Polish nationalist who emigrated from Poland to Paris after the failed uprising of 1830 was Frédéric Chopin, the famous composer who took romantic piano music to new heights. Although he never returned to Poland, some of his best compositions were expressions of a deep spirit of Polish patriotism, especially his polonaises and mazurkas. In 1834 Poland's most famous Romantic poet, Adam Mickiewicz, wrote his immortal *Pan Tadeusz.* The first line of the epic poem was addressed to his country: "O my Lithuania [Poland-Lithuania], You are like health itself. Only someone who has lost You can ever fully appreciate You."

In the second half of the nineteenth century, Poles experienced a new and even more dangerous threat. Otto von Bismarck of Prussia, who had succeeded in uniting Germany in 1870 and 1871, pursued a policy of "Germanization" of his Polish territories. This meant that Bismarck, now chancellor of Germany, wanted to eliminate all Polish culture and tradition from his Polish provinces and make loyal German citizens out of future Polish generations. The Polish language was forbidden in all official institutions. Even school instruction was given only in German. Everywhere, Polish history and culture were banned.

There was a similar campaign to implement a policy of "Russification" of those Polish territories under the control of the Russian czars. In those areas students were expelled from school simply for talking to one another in Polish.

Despite these obstacles, however, Polish language and culture survived. This was due in large part to the deep religious faith of the Poles. Since Poland did not exist as an independent state for almost 123 years, it was the church that preserved Polish culture and tradition during the partition period of Polish history. The Catholic church thus became for many Poles an alternate social institution to which they owed their first loyalty. The church helped to maintain a sense of Polish national identity.

But the Germanization and Russification of the late nineteenth century were much more than just an attack upon Polish statehood. These policies threatened to take away the very Polishness of the people. In the struggle of

Poles to maintain their Polishness, Catholicism became even more closely associated with national identity. This did not bode well for non-Catholic inhabitants of Poland, especially Jews.

It was only in the Austrian partition sector that the policy of forced cultural assimilation of Poles was not followed. For one thing, the Austrians themselves were Roman Catholic. And in 1867 the Austrians even granted their Polish territories a limited measure of self-rule, or autonomy. The trouble here was not political suppression but rather economic hardship. The Austrian sector, known as Galicia, was one of the poorest provinces in Europe. The phrase "Galician misery" became a standard reference to extreme rural poverty. The root of the problem was underdevelopment. Galician industrial development was ignored at a time when many other parts of Europe were going through an industrial revolution. This lack of employment opportunities in urban factories resulted in a severe overpopulation in the countryside. There were too many mouths to feed and not enough land for growing food. The Polish peasant in Galicia could no longer make a living from the land. In the late nineteenth and early twentieth centuries, thousands of Galician Poles left their homes to search for a better life in the Western Hemisphere. Most of them came to America.

POLAND REBORN

As long as Poland's two most powerful neighbors, Russia to the east and Germany to the west, remained united in their commitment to keep Polish territories under their control, Poland's fight for political freedom was doomed to failure. The combined force of both of these powers was too great an obstacle for the Poles to overcome. The inclusion of Austria-Hungary to the south as a third partition power bent on preserving the status quo made the task of seeking independence even more difficult. For almost 125 years, this triple alliance of Russia, Germany, and Austria kept Poland divided.

In the early twentieth century, however, things began to change on the international scene. This would have profound implications for Poland. Polish hopes for independence were rekindled when it appeared that the long-standing alliance between Russia and Germany might finally come to an end. Nationalism in the Balkan peninsula, especially in Serbia, had fueled intense hatreds that threatened to upset the existing balance of power relationships. A spirit of aggressive militarism and competition for overseas colonies added to the war fever. The result was the outbreak of the Great War in 1914. Poland's conquerors went to war against one another. As World War I began, Russia was fighting on one side of the war, allied with France and Great Britain. Germany was fighting on the other side, allied with Austria-Hungary.

It is impossible to describe adequately the horror that World War I brought to Poland. The Poles were caught in the middle of the conflict. Much of the fighting and physical destruction took place on Polish soil, simply because Poland was geographically situated between Russia and Germany. Of course, Poland did not formally exist at the time. It had been incorporated into the political boundaries of the partitioning powers as German or Russian territories inhabited by Polish-speaking peoples. About half of the Polish lands belonged to Germany and Austria-Hungary. Roughly an equal amount of Polish land was under Russian domination.

The main question for Poles was: With whom should they ally themselves politically? Long before World War I, Poles were divided into two opposing political camps on this issue. One camp, led by Roman Dmowski, felt that Germany was the main enemy of the Polish people. The other camp, led by Józef Piłsudski, felt that the Russian threat was more dangerous. The dilemma was a real one. Both countries had territorial designs on Polish territory, but Poles could not hope to fight both countries at the same time. On this point, at least, Piłsudski and Dmowski agreed.

And what happened to the Poles during the Great War? For whom did they actually fight? Both Russia and Germany had drafted soldiers from their Polish territories into their armies. The result was a tragic situation for the Polish people. Poles from the Russian territories were forced to fight for Russia; Poles from the German territories were forced to fight on the side of Germany. In other words, Poles fought against Poles in World War I, killing one another in the name of foreign enemies who had been responsible for destroying Poland's independence. It was a nightmare. In some cases, Poles actually fought in battles against their own relatives who lived in another partition sector of what had been Poland.

Despite the horrors of 1914 to 1918, the end of World War I brought with it hope for a rebirth of Poland's statehood. The leaders of the world had gathered outside Paris at the Palace of Versailles to discuss the terms for ending the war. Many of them saw a clear advantage in having a Polish buffer state between Germany and Russia. The French and the Americans proved to be the strongest supporters of efforts to resurrect the Polish nation. U.S. President Woodrow Wilson presented his famous list of Fourteen Points as a guide for ending the war. One of them (Point Thirteen) called for the reestablishment of an independent Poland in those "territories inhabited by indisputably Polish populations," and assurance to Poland of a "free and secure access to the sea."[5]

A buffer state would be created by allowing the former Polish territories of Germany, Austria-Hungary, and Russia to be reunited once more as an independent Poland. Access to the Baltic Sea was achieved by the inclusion of the so-called Polish Corridor, lands that Germany had controlled during the partition period. Lech Walesa's port city of Gdansk, known also as Danzig, was not included within the new borders of Poland. Because of its large German population, it was allowed to remain a so-called free city.

It was a relatively simple matter to take Polish territories away from recently defeated Germany and Austria-Hungary. This could be justified as their price for losing the war. But what about Russia? It had been an ally of France, Britain, and the United States during the war. How could its Polish territories now be given away? However, an unusual twist of circumstances had occurred in Russia. This would prove favorable to the cause of Polish statehood. During the war, a revolution in Russia had overthrown the Russian czar in March 1917. The Bolshevik, or Communist, party leader, Lenin, had become the new head of the country by November 1917. He quickly pulled Russia out of the war by signing a peace treaty with the still undefeated Germany. In the process he gave up to Germany considerable territories, including Polish territories formerly under Russian domination. This infuriated Russia's former allies, who after 1918 were not inclined to return any territory, Polish or otherwise, to Lenin's Communist Russia.

Resurrected at the end of World War I, Poland had finally regained its independence. Poland was reborn as a democratic state—a republic that proclaimed political freedoms guaranteeing a measure of political participation by the people. It was a proud moment for Poles, and there was much cheering and jubilation. Yet the battle was only half over. The nearly 125 years of foreign domination had created huge problems, and enormous difficulties still had to be overcome. Poland had been divided under three separate economic and political systems, and had developed accordingly. It would not be easy to make Poland whole again. Even the railroad tracks in one sector were not the same size as those in the others. And that was just the beginning. As one writer points out, "Poland became independent with six currencies, four official Army languages, eighteen registered political parties . . . three legal codes, three disparate codes of social behavior, and regions (such as industrially important Silesia) with administrations separate from the central authority."[6]

Undaunted, Poles embarked on a huge effort to recreate their own national heritage. They made tremendous strides in the twenty years following the end of World War I (1918). Their prime concern was the establishment of a single currency, a single legal code, and a single central administration. Also, since Gdansk was declared a free city by the terms of the peace treaty, Poland had no real port of its own on the Baltic. So it built a new port city slightly to the west of

Gdansk. Within a few years Gdynia had become a thriving port.

But the effort to build a new nation was cut short by the German invasion of Poland on September 1, 1939. This event triggered World War II when Great Britain and France, in fulfillment of their alliance agreements, declared war on Germany. By the terms of a secret German-Soviet pact, the Soviet Union participated in the aggression into Polish territories. Stalin's troops occupied Poland's eastern territories on September 17, 1939. Once again, after only twenty short years of independence, Poland had lost its freedom. After military victories in Western Europe, the Germans soon turned on their former Soviet partner, and Hitler attacked the Soviet Union in June 1941. German domination of Poland lasted until 1945, when the Western allies, including the Soviet Union, succeeded in liberating Poland from the grip of Hitler's armies.

WORLD WAR II AND ITS EFFECTS

The defeat of Nazi Germany and the victory of the Soviet Union in East Central Europe at the end of World War II brought many profound social changes. Poland, like other countries in the region, was radically transformed in a number of fundamental ways. Most significantly, it was brought into the Soviet political and military sphere of influence. The leader of the Soviet Union, Joseph Stalin, had proven to be a formidable foe both during and after the war. Largely through his influence and power during the postwar conferences with the allies (especially at Yalta and Potsdam), the Soviet Union gained relatively free rein in East Central Europe.

Soviet troops had liberated this region from German occupation. Since they were already present militarily, and had remained in a relatively high state of mobilization after the war, they were not about to pull out anytime soon. More than anything else, the presence of the huge Red Army, as the Soviet army was called, ensured Stalin's political victory in East Central Europe. Perhaps it was naive on the part of the

Allies, led by President Franklin Delano Roosevelt of the United States, to believe in Stalin's promise of freedom of national self-determination and free elections for Poland. On the other hand, the only real alternative would have meant war with the Soviet Union. No one wanted the extremely heavy Allied casualties that would have resulted. The price to ensure the freedom of East Central Europe in any absolute terms was deemed too high. It was easier to hope that Stalin would live up to at least some of the promises he had made about freedom for Poland.[7] But many Poles felt betrayed by the willingness of the Allies to defer to Stalin's domination of East Central Europe.

The result was clear from the standpoint of Polish history. Stalin soon made a mockery of the term "national self-determination." Within a short period after the victory of the Allies in Europe in May 1945, Stalin had succeeded in bringing a Communist government into power; this would never have happened without him. The so-called Lublin government, set up in the Polish city of Lublin, was in reality a puppet government for Moscow. On paper Poland was a free nation, but in actuality its independence was lost once again.

Of course, when it became clear that Stalin was not about to live up to his promise of free elections and national self-determination for Poland, the allies strongly protested. Harry S. Truman was now president of the United States, which supported the London-based Polish government-in-exile. Truman's sharp verbal attacks on Moscow's handling of the Polish situation caused an international crisis. But the Allies did not take any direct military action, and the crisis in East Central Europe marked the beginning of the Cold War between the United States and the Soviet Union.

The Communist party of Poland, known as the PZPR, was the key link to the Soviet Union. This party was allied with and supportive of the Communist party of the Soviet Union headed by Stalin. Through frequent communication as well as occasional meetings between the leaders of these two parties, Stalin and his successors made known their wishes as to what was and was not acceptable domestic and foreign policy. In this way, the Soviet Union directed the internal affairs of Poland and other Eastern bloc nations. Although Poland's leaders often argued for their own points and did resist certain demands made by Moscow, the overall picture was clearly established: Poland was to remain firmly embedded in the Soviet sphere of influence. With regard to foreign policy, Poland would have to toe the Moscow line, and with regard to its internal development, it would be forced to adopt socialism and Marxist economic policy. Any attempt by Poland, or any other Soviet satellite state, to break out of this mold would be met by harsh retaliation from the ever-present Red Army.

ETHNIC AND RELIGIOUS UNIFORMITY

Another of the main changes that occurred in Poland after World War II was that the country became ethnically and religiously homogeneous, or uniform. In other words, Poland became almost exclusively inhabited by Polish-speaking Catholics. This had not been the case in the past. Significant numbers of non-Polish ethnic minorities and non–Roman Catholics had always been present in Polish history. They included sizable numbers of Ukrainians, Lithuanians, Germans, Byelorussians, Jews, and Gypsies as well as smaller numbers of many other nationalities or ethnic minorities. Two related factors caused a sudden and drastic alteration of this situation. The terrible deportations and the casualties inflicted by the Germans during World War II and the boundary shifts immediately after the war were largely responsible for eliminating these other groups from Polish territories.

A tragic story is that of the Polish Jews, who before the start of World War II numbered approximately 3.5 million; by 1945 the number of Polish Jews still living in Poland had been reduced to less than thirty thousand.[8] Some had succeeded in escaping from the German persecution by fleeing Poland just prior to or during the war. Millions who were not so lucky perished at Auschwitz or the dozens of other concentration camps set up by the Germans on Polish soil. At this time, many thousands of Polish Gypsies were also killed in the gas chambers of these camps. Many of the Polish Jews who survived by fleeing Poland were reluctant to return to Poland after the war. Many of the Polish Jews who survived the war left Poland. And after the government established anti-Semitic policies, many Polish Jews permanently emigrated from Poland, most of them going to Israel and the United States. A major exodus occurred in 1968. At the present time, there are about four thousand Jews living in Poland.

The ethnic and religious composition of Poland was also affected by boundary shifts after the war. In one of the largest planned mass emigration projects in history, the map of Poland was redrawn after World War II. Millions of people were forced to move from their homes in order to accommodate to the new boundaries. Once again, Stalin's actions forced the situation. At the Yalta and Potsdam conferences, Stalin persuaded the allies to agree to new national boundaries for Poland. The idea was to take about one-third of the entire Polish state, namely the land lying to the east, and incorporate it into the Soviet Union. This territory was inhabited largely by people who were not ethnically Polish, a fact that was used to justify such an action. Lithuanians and Byelorussians made up the vast majority of the population in the northern part of this land, while Ukrainians dominated in the southern regions. Both of these regions were incorporated into the Soviet Union as new republics.

At the same time, at the expense of Germany, Polish territory was substantially increased on its western border. Lech Walesa's free port of Gdansk also became part of the Polish state. This loss of territory was part of Germany's punishment for starting the war. Much of this land had at one time in the past been a part of the Polish state, a fact that served to help justify this action in world opinion. The lands acquired by Poland from Germany were thus called the regained territories (*ziemia odzyskana*). German inhabitants of this land were forced to emigrate to the remaining German lands, and Polish citizens were brought in to occupy this new territory. Many state farms were set up here as socialist agricultural enterprises. Much land was also given outright to Polish citizens, who in this way suddenly became private landowners. They occupied the houses and public buildings the Germans had left behind, and they took over the cultivation of the fields.

Thus, war casualties and postwar boundary shifts created an ethnically and religiously homogeneous Poland as it entered the postwar, Communist phase of its history.

COMMUNIST POLAND

The Polish Communists are those who in 1945 took the factories from the capitalists and to this day have forgotten to give them to the workers.

POLISH POLITICAL JOKE IN THE 1970s

THE SOVIET MODEL OF SOCIALISM

After World War II, Poland and other countries of East Central Europe were brought into the political orbit of the Soviet Union, which was ruled by Stalin and the Communist party. Because these countries were dominated by the Soviet Union, they became known in the West as the Soviet bloc, or the Soviet satellite states. They officially referred to themselves, however, as members of the Warsaw Pact, an international alliance agreement signed in Warsaw. Poland thus became a socialist country based upon the Soviet model. It was officially called the People's Republic of Poland, or PRL (Polska Rzeczypospolita Ludowa).

Soviet-style socialism had its roots in the ideas of Karl Marx, a German social philosopher and revolutionary. Marx had spent most of his life analyzing capitalism, an economic system based on the private ownership of the means of production—the factories, tools, equipment, and so on necessary for the production of goods. In capitalism, the owners of the factories, the capitalists, would make a profit by hiring workers to produce goods, which would then be sold in the marketplace. Marx felt that the factory workers, as an entire social group, or class, were being taken advantage of by the capitalists, who were getting rich from the hard labor of the workers. Marx saw this condition leading to an inevitable struggle between these two social classes. On the one hand, there was the bourgeoisie, the rich and powerful capitalist class, the ruling elite of society. On the other hand, there was the proletariat, the downtrodden class of workers who had little wealth and even less political power. The struggle, as Marx saw it, was therefore one between the haves and the have-nots of society, between the oppressors and the oppressed, between the ruling elite and the powerless poor.

According to Marx, when the laws of history demanded it, workers would unite, start a revolution, overthrow the capitalists, and seize control of their factories. After all, the workers were many and the capitalists were few. All the workers together would now own the factories. This would mean the end of private ownership of the means of production—in other words, the end of capitalism—and the beginning of socialism, or the collective (public) ownership of the factories. Once this happened, according to Marx, exploitation of the workers would cease, since there would no longer be any upper class exploiting the lower class. And who would lead the workers to unite and start a revolution? The Communist party, of course, as the vanguard of the proletariat, would lead the workers to a socialist transformation of society. In time, social classes would disappear entirely, and a classless society would arise. Marx called this final stage "communism," and he believed that it would bring with it social equality and justice.

It is important to realize that although Soviet-style socialism was based upon the ideas of Karl Marx, it was not identical to them. From the very beginning, Marx's ideas were adapted by Lenin, leader of the Bolshevik (Communist) party, to fit Russia's specific historical circumstances and Lenin's own political designs. To Lenin and the Bolshevik party, power became more important than theory, and when the two were at odds, Marx's theory was sacrificed. Stalin, as Lenin's political successor, continued and accelerated this pattern. In doing so, Stalin, under the guise of Marxism, transformed the Soviet Union into a dictatorship.

In effect, Stalin's version of socialism meant that the Communist Party had a "monopoly of political power, purges, terror, concentration camps, planned industrialization, and collectivization."[1] Stalin ruled the Soviet Union with a brutal hand until his death in 1953. Millions starved to death under his economic policies; many thousands were murdered for their political views or were sent to concentration camps in Siberia. Unless one has lived through it, one cannot truly understand the terror that was felt during the Stalinist purges. A political anecdote attempts to present a picture of the overall mood of the Stalinist period.

An American, a Pole, and a Russian are trading stories about the happiest day in each of their lives. The American begins, "It was when I became president of my company after twenty years of hard work." The Pole looks on sadly, knowing his story is not nearly as good. "The happiest day of my life," he says, "was when I finally earned enough money, after twenty years of scrimping and saving, to buy a Polish Fiat 126P"—a very modest car by Western standards. The Russian then gives his version: "The happiest day of my life was about five years ago. I'll never forget it. It was about two A.M. The wife and I were in bed asleep. The kids were sleeping next to us, as we could only afford a one-room flat. Suddenly there was a knock at the door. Two men in long overcoats showed me their IDs as members of Stalin's internal security police. One of them asked me, 'Are you Ivan Ivanovich?' 'No.' I sighed. 'Mr. Ivanovich lives one floor below.' "

It was Stalin's version of socialism that reached Poland and the other satellite states after 1945. And it arrived in East Central Europe along a much different path than Marx had predicted. There had been no socialist rebellion of the workers in Poland, no revolutionary upsurge against capitalism. Socialism was not something Polish workers had freely chosen for themselves; it was forced upon them by a foreign power that had long threatened Poland's freedom. For this reason it was hard for Poles to make a clear distinction between being anti-Russian (anti-Soviet) and anti-socialist (anti-Communist). For many Poles they were one and the same thing. Two political jokes that were very popular in Poland illustrate this problem.

An army officer from the Soviet Union is touring Polish schools. He asks a little boy in the fourth grade, "Who is your father?" The boy replies, "Stalin." The officer asks him to explain. "Stalin is the spiritual father of all of us," the little boy replies. "Very good," says the officer. "And who is your mother?" The boy has learned his lessons well. "The Communist party is my mother. She is the mother of all of us." Pleased with the boy's responses, the officer asks further, "And what do you want to be when you grow up?" "An orphan," the boy replies.

A teacher asks a student in a seventh grade history class, "What kind of Poland do we have now?" The student replies, "People's Poland." The teacher continues, "Good! How else can you describe it?" "Democratic Poland," comes the student's next response. "Yes, and what else?" "Socialist Poland." The teacher continues the history lesson. "Very nice. And what kind of Poland did we have before the war?" The student thinks for a second and then answers, "A free and independent Poland."

The Soviet economic model called for a planned economy. The state, not the private entrepreneur or business owner, would decide what, how, and how much was to be produced and how it was to be distributed. Specifically, the Soviet model for the socialist transformation of society depended upon two things: the rapid industrialization of the country and the collectivization of agriculture (the combining of small peasant farms into much larger cooperative farms). This economic model was also applied to Poland and the other countries of East Central Europe under Stalin's political control. Shortly after the war, the Communist leadership of Poland began a program of rapid industrialization. The aim was to transform the country from a backward agricultural nation to a modern industrialized one. Unlike Western economic development, however, industrialization in East Central Europe was to be accomplished within a socialist, not a capitalist, framework. This meant that the state, not private business owners or corporations, owned the means of production.

There has been considerable confusion as to whether Poland and the other Soviet bloc nations should have been called "socialist" or "Communist." First, no Soviet bloc nation considered itself to be truly Communist. Rather, they all claimed to be representatives of a socialist economy in the process of gradual transition to pure communism. In such a future condition, there would no longer be any social classes. People would contribute to society whatever they were able and would get back from society whatever they needed, according to this formula: "From each according to his ability, to each according to his need." Moreover, there would be no need for a political apparatus such as the state, since, according to Karl Marx, the state had arisen in the first place only to protect and defend the interests of the ruling class. Once the continued development of socialism had finally eliminated social classes, the state would simply wither away. Communism, therefore, was an ideal condition that no country had yet reached.

Nevertheless, political parties around the world could, and frequently did, label themselves "Communist." This simply meant that they were followers of the ideology of Karl Marx and Soviet-style socialism. In Poland the Communist party was officially called the Polish United Workers party or the PZPR. Such a political party might establish a socialist economy which, in accordance with Marxist theory, would eventually lead to true communism. But since the Communist parties of East Central Europe actually held political power, these nations were referred to in the West as Communist countries. In short, from a political viewpoint they could be called Communist, but in terms of their economic system they were socialist.

In each country of East Central Europe the Soviet model was applied somewhat differently. The pace of change would sometimes be slower, sometimes faster. Sometimes certain deviations from the model would be allowed in particular countries for particular reasons. This was especially true after the death of Stalin in 1953. Poland was somewhat unusual in the Soviet bloc for the degree to which it was allowed to deviate from the Soviet model. This came to be referred to as the "Polish road to socialism." Only part of the economic system of Poland was socialist in the standard definition of the term: "the public ownership of the means of production." The industrial sector of the economy could certainly be called socialist, as over 90 percent of large industry was owned and operated directly by the state. This pertained both to prewar factories that were nationalized (taken over by the state) and to the numerous factories built after the war under Communist party supervision. However, over 80 percent of the farmland was still privately owned by individual peasant households at the time Lech Walesa led the striking workers of Gdansk.

After World War II, Poland did make an attempt to socialize agriculture by setting up state-owned collective farms based on the Soviet model. But this policy was extremely unpopular among the rural inhabitants. Productivity on these collectives was also very low. Three years after Stalin's death, they were allowed to disband voluntarily. Most of the land returned to private ownership. The breakup of the collective farms and the return to private agriculture made Poland unique in the Soviet bloc.[2]

The Polish system, therefore, represented a mixing of Soviet-style socialism with a bit of leftover capitalism. It combined government- or state-owned industry with private agriculture and private land ownership. The peasants, for their part, were hostile to any program that even faintly threatened the removal of the land from their personal ownership.

They remained very mistrustful of governmental policies, a fact that did not bode well for Polish agriculture in the long run. And as long as the ultimate aim of official Communist party policy was couched in terms of socialism, the peasants could never really feel secure. The government had tried to take their land away before, and it just might try to do it again.

ECONOMIC STAGNATION AND SOCIAL DISCONTENT

The socialist economic system of Poland failed to provide an acceptable standard of living for most Poles in the postwar period. Social unrest, which eventually led to the birth of the Solidarity movement in 1980, ultimately grew out of that failure. A Polish sociologist, Wladyslaw Kwasniewicz, once commented that the "workers cared more about ham than ideology."[3] He meant that most people were not absolutely opposed to socialism in Poland as long as it could provide them with the good life. People were more interested in whether they could put food on the table for their children than in philosophical distinctions about the nature of the "ism" they were living under, whether it was capitalism or socialism. If the socialist system had provided the Polish people with a reasonable standard of living, comparable to one found in the West, the people could have lived under a socialist system ruled by the Communist party; if that had happened, Solidarity would never have been born. The Polish sociologist continued, "It is no coincidence that all of the major social protests began when the government raised the prices of consumer goods, especially food prices."[4]

While this last statement is certainly true, Poles were not just concerned with economic or material interests. Certainly, the weak economy most angered the workers, but other factors should not be ignored. Poles could never have completely accepted Russian domination of Poland. The issue of freedom was not a separate question apart from economic concerns. Poles felt that if they had true independence, and true freedom to develop their own economy without Soviet interference, they would have been able to solve their economic problems. Russian domination, Poles felt, was at the root of the economic crisis. The initials of the Polish Communist party, PZPR, were mockingly read by Poles to stand for: Party Always Supporting Russia (Partia Zawsze Popierająca Rosję).

The logic was very clear in the Polish mind: The Russians controlled the Communist party of the Soviet Union. The Communist party of the Soviet Union controlled the Communist party of Poland. The Communist party of Poland controlled the Polish government. And the Polish government controlled the Polish economy. Thus, to the average Pole, the real enemy was Russia. Economics, politics, and international power relations were all interrelated and inseparable.

Would Poles have accepted socialism if it had provided them with material well-being? An old Polish proverb seems to address this point: "If my aunt had a mustache, she would have been my uncle." In other words, if Polish-style socialism could have produced a Western-style economy, it would have done so. But then it would not have been Polish-style socialism; it would have been something else. And what did the Poles themselves think about capitalism? Many expressed it in the form of a political joke: "According to Marxist theory, is it true that capitalism is dying? Yes, it is true, but we, too, would like such a death."

Polish workers saw their lives going nowhere under the existing socialist economic system. The good life promised under socialism never came, and economic hardships even increased. Lines at the state-owned shops got longer and longer, and the quality and quantity of the goods available did not come close to keeping up with the demand. This complaint was frequently heard: "So many pigs in Poland, yet the stores have no ham." Several times a week, workers saw their wives and parents standing in front of stores for hours in order to purchase staples that were readily available in the West. This contrast with the West was a constant reminder that their own system was inadequate. It was commonplace throughout Poland to see people standing in line at 4:00 A.M. in front of a food store that would open at 9:00 A.M., at which time they might find out that the meat delivery would come around 11:00 A.M.

So if Poland, still largely an agricultural country, had so many pigs, what was happening to all the ham? The answer to this question was not one the workers wanted to hear. Some meat products, to be sure, were going to the Soviet Union. But a substantial amount was going to those Western capitalist countries like France, West Germany, and the United States, whose economic policies the Poles admired so much. The importation of Western technology into Poland was essential for its continued industrial development. Poland had little to offer the West in return. Food, therefore, became a prime export and source of revenue. The government bought meat from the Polish farmers at relatively low prices and sold it to the West for hard cash. Only a relatively small amount of this meat was allocated for distribution at home. Thus the meat shortage was artificially created by government economic policies.

Not surprisingly, most Poles held the government leadership responsible for the economic shortcomings. But through it all, the people kept their sense of humor. Since public criticism of state policies was not allowed, popular disdain for Communist policies was often expressed in the form of political jokes that made their way through Poland very rapidly. Dozens of these jokes were constantly circulating throughout Poland. Since open public criticism of the Communist government was still rather dangerous and could easily lead to the loss of a job (as Lech Walesa found out on more than one occasion), political jokes became an outlet for social protest. Although public speech was censored, Poles were not afraid to express their true feelings privately, among friends and acquaintances. Here are some political jokes that clearly expressed the people's dissatisfaction with the economic policies of the Communist government and its leaders.

People have been waiting in line for ham for over four hours. Finally one man announces, "That's it. I've had it. This is all the fault of Gierek, our illustrious leader of the Communist party. I'm going to Warsaw and kick him right in the butt." The next day the man meekly returns to his old place in the meat line, which has now moved up only a few feet. He sees the same people next to him, still waiting in line. They ask him with intense curiosity, "Well, tell us what happened in Warsaw? Did you kick Gierek in the butt or what?" "No," the man replies. "That line was even longer than the meat line."

One man asks another as they are riding in a trolley, "What is the difference between the government and a piece of used toilet paper?" The other replies, "Actually, there is no difference at all. They're both full of crap." Suddenly two men in plainclothes who have been eavesdropping show their badges as members of the internal security police. One of them says, "What's the difference between this trolley and you two gentlemen? Simple, the trolley is going on ahead, but you two are going down to the police station with us. You are both under arrest." During the subsequent questioning, the policeman says to one of them, "Don't deny it. We heard you say that the government is full of crap." The man protests in vain, "But, Officer, I was referring to the American capitalist government, not the Polish socialist government." The policeman replies haughtily, "Oh, so you think you can put one over on us, huh, buddy? Well, it won't work. We know damn well which government is full of crap."

As if to add insult to injury, the state-determined wages of the workers were too low to cover the average cost of living. A popular maxim said that Polish workers were paid too much to starve to death, but not enough to live on. The average family had to have some additional source of income, and *kombinacja* became a fact of life. Literally, this word means "combination," but it was used to refer to a sort of wheeling-and-dealing mode of life, a cleverness that a person needed to make connections and social contacts in order to get extra money, goods, or services. Illegal activities on the black market, bribery, stealing on the job, granting special favors to friends or relatives, moonlighting, and so on were a few of the many forms of *kombinacja*.

Sometimes the income from this wheeling and dealing

exceeded a family's official income. Poles would joke: "I make four thousand zloty a month. I spend six thousand zloty a month. And the difference I put in the bank to save up for a car." But even if a typical Pole had put his or her entire income in the bank every month and did not spend anything at all, it would still have taken about eight years to buy a modest car such as a Polish Fiat. Waiting times for a telephone often averaged ten years, while getting an apartment could take much longer. *Kombinacja* became a way around the bureaucratic impasses of the system. Poles frequently neglected their state jobs while they were busy wheeling and dealing, often during working hours. Did they feel guilty about this? "No," came the answer. "The state pretends to pay us, so we pretend to work."

Many jobs, however, did not allow workers the luxury of "combination." They were grueling and tiresome, and employees had to work very hard. These people grew even more resentful. They watched others exploit the system for their own personal benefit while they had little to show for their labor except empty government promises for the future.

THE RED BOURGEOISIE

Poles saw a huge difference between what the Communist government told them and what it actually did. This gulf between the high ideals of socialist theory and the dire realities of everyday life was the source of much popular antagonism toward the government. The workers were fully aware of the hypocrisy in the existing system. While they struggled just to put food on their tables, they watched the Communist party elite build private houses in the countryside and buy food and consumer items at special stores in which the common person could not afford to shop or was not allowed to enter. Many Poles deeply resented the privileges of the *nomenklatura*, the 200,000 or so Communist party members, managers, and upper-level bureaucrats in a country of approximately 34 million. Not everyone was being asked to sacrifice equally. It seemed to an increasing number of Poles that the Communist party, instead of representing the interests of the working class, had itself become the new ruling class. The phrase "red bourgeoisie" was commonly heard on the streets.

This term was especially biting. The bourgeoisie was the term Marx used for the capitalist class that had exploited the working class by forcing them to work for survival wages. In the meantime the wealthy capitalists lived high off the hog on all the profit the workers' labor had produced. "Red," of course, was the symbolic color of the Communist revolution that was supposed to end this exploitation. The Communist party, the representative of the working class, would overthrow the capitalists and set up a workers' state in which capitalist exploitation would be eliminated. The term "red bourgeoisie" therefore implied that the Communist party elite, the supposed representatives of the workers, were really the new masters. They were asking the workers to sacrifice while they themselves were living the good life. This was one of the political points made by George Orwell in *Animal Farm*, a book well known in Poland for its highly critical view of Soviet-style communism. Underground copies in Polish had been circulating for some time, and Poles applied its most famous lines to their own lives. Under socialism, people were supposed to be equal, but under Soviet-sponsored, Polish socialism "some people were more equal than others."

Many Poles became pessimistic and felt there was no hope for the future. Many of them found ways to leave Poland and then asked for political asylum once they were in the West. Others, like Lech Walesa, remained in Poland and continued to struggle, still believing that their actions could make a difference.

THE CHURCH IN COMMUNIST POLAND

After World War II, as we have seen, Poland was inhabited almost completely by people who thought of themselves as ethnically Polish and who were Roman Catholic. At the same time, however, Poland's government was dominated by men who were avowed atheists. This, of course, was a fundamental part of Communist philosophy. Karl Marx had referred to organized religion as the "opiate of the masses." By this he meant that religious beliefs were used by the ruling elite of a society to keep the common people from starting a revolt against their rulers. Marx felt that religion, by manipulating the minds of the citizens, was teaching people to accept their low place in society; this prevented them from rising up against their oppressors. Since atheism was entrenched in Marxist philosophy, the leaders of the Communist party of the Soviet Union, and by extension the leaders of its satellite states in East Central Europe, could not claim to be anything else. Somewhat paradoxically, Poland in 1945 became a country populated almost entirely by Roman Catholics but ruled by Marxist atheists.

The fundamental incompatibility of atheism and Catholicism was bound to cause social tension. This showed up in many forms in the social and political life of the country. First of all, it immediately gave rise to open hostility and potential conflict between the Catholic church and the Communist party. The church was a direct threat to the legitimacy of the party. The church had the open loyalty of the people and enjoyed immense popular support. And the church's philosophical position, announced in a public forum every time holy mass was celebrated, was itself an attack upon the theoretical underpinnings of the Communist party. The church proclaimed the glory of God; the Communists denied God's very existence. The church was thus a constant thorn in the side of the Communist government, a festering wound that refused to heal as long as the thorn was not removed.

On the other hand, the party was a direct threat to the existence of the Catholic church. There could be no greater threat to the church than a government which proclaimed that God did not exist. The elimination of all religious institutions had been made a fundamental part of the Communist party platform in the Soviet Union. The earlier attack upon the Russian Orthodox church by the Soviet Communists had been extremely harsh. Since the ultimate aim of communism was to bring an end to these "old-fashioned" religious beliefs, there was always the danger that the same fate might eventually befall the Catholic church in Poland.

In the Communist period, the Black Madonna became an unofficial symbol of the struggle of the Polish people against Russian domination and Soviet-imposed communism. The message was quite clear: "With the help of the Virgin Mary we will overcome all adversity. She will help save us again as she has in the past." It was a message of hope, a message of love, a religious message first and foremost, but one with definite political overtones. In the postwar period, a Polish Cardinal, Stefan Wyszynski, called the Black Madonna "the queen of Poland." Replicas of the painting were carried around at special processions at certain times of the year. Every village, every small town, sometimes even every apartment complex, had its own Black Madonna celebration. Often the Madonna would move from home to home and apartment to apartment, spending a night or so at each place on ornately decorated altars set up specially for the occasion. One of the homes that the Black Madonna regularly visited was that of Lech Walesa and his family.

But despite their total incompatibility, party and church were not ready for all-out war. Neither side was strong enough to achieve a total victory, and each had too much to lose. During the Stalinist period, from 1945 to 1956, the authorities in Poland did step up their attacks on the church. They even succeeded in forcing a number of concessions from frightened bishops. But government policy failed to undermine the church, mainly because of the keen political sense of Cardinal Stefan Wyszynski, primate (or first cardinal) of Poland. He was arrested and imprisoned in 1953 during the Stalinist repression, but was freed in 1956.

Cardinal Wyszynski saw to it that the Catholic church was able to maintain its unity in the struggle to survive in a totalitarian system. Under severe pressure from the government, certain bishops had made remarks that seemed to implicate the church in spying for foreign governments. Wyszynski refused to play into the hands of the authorities. He refused to condemn Polish bishops for their remarks. A long period of silent accommodation and compromise resulted. The church was to stay out of political affairs, and the government would not interfere with the private worship of its citizens. As it turned out, neither side was able to keep its promise completely. The government would simply have to wait for the new socialist society to produce human beings who saw the folly of organized religion. Eventually, so went the official party line, with the socialist evolution of society, and the appearance of the "new Communist citizen," the church would simply die out. As it turned out, it was the other way around.

THE QUESTION OF LEGITIMACY

Each society develops its own idea of moral force. The Catholic church in Poland, in its opposition to Communist atheism, was a moral force in the society. So, too, were the people's value judgments and assessments as to what constituted a legitimate government. This issue of political legitimacy is crucial to the understanding of social change not only in Poland but in all the Soviet bloc nations of East Central Europe. Legitimacy is the recognized right of a given organization or group to exercise political power in a country. It is what makes the difference between power and authority. Power is brute force; it is the ability to get others to do what we want them to do. Authority is legitimate power, power that people accept and acknowledge as right and proper. For example, if a man comes into a classroom waving a gun and tells us to leave the building, we are likely to comply. But we do so out of fear, not because we feel he has the right to order us around. If the same man is wearing a fireman's uniform, we are likely to feel that he has a right to order us out of the building.

Similarly, if a government is considered legitimate, then people generally believe it has a moral right to exercise power, and they will be likely to obey its orders. In Poland and the other nations of the Soviet bloc, however, the power of the government was based more on force than on recognition of a moral right to rule. Stalin had forced these countries to accept the rule of the Communist party. This created a very low level of political legitimacy and made it very difficult for these governments to rule effectively. Their power was based on force alone.

The governments of East Central Europe did try to win the hearts and the minds of the people by extensive propaganda campaigns. Signs on factory walls, bridges, and dining halls praised the virtues of the Communist-ruled state. The immediate purpose of the propaganda was to show how good the government was and to demonstrate the superiority of the Communist system. The ultimate aim of the propaganda, however, was to convince the people that Communist authority was just and proper. In this way the government hoped to bring a greater sense of legitimacy to its rule. The leaders knew that without a certain minimum level of popular moral support, it would be difficult for the government to survive indefinitely, no matter how strong it was militarily.

But propaganda alone did not convince the people of East Central Europe. This was especially true in Poland. The government's legitimacy would hang on its ability to provide the basic necessities of life to its people. Performance, not propaganda, was the real yardstick by which the people measured the legitimacy of their government. A political joke that was very popular in Poland in the 1970s, when Leonid Brezhnev was the head of the Soviet Union, serves to demonstrate the forced nature of political obedience in Communist Poland.

One morning Brezhnev walks out onto his balcony in the Kremlin and the sun, which is just beginning to rise, says to him: "Good morning, Comrade Leonid, first secretary of our illustrious Communist party, and leader of our people. How are you this morning?" Brezhnev replies, "Thank you, Mr. Sun, for your lovely words," and goes back inside. A little past noontime Brezhnev returns to the balcony and the sun repeats its greeting. In the late afternoon, just as the sun is beginning to set, Brezhnev returns to the balcony once again. But now there is total silence. After waiting in vain for the sun to bestow its praise upon him again, Brezhnev gets impatient and shouts, "Mr. Sun, why don't you greet me and praise me as you did twice before?" The sun replies abruptly, "Kiss my backside, Leonid. I'm in the West now."

A personal incident comes to mind that also illustrates the low level of political legitimacy in Communist-ruled Poland. In 1976 I was in Poland doing research. While I was interviewing a peasant family in a village near the town of Legnica in southwest Poland, I was struck by the naive and idealistic view many Poles had of the United States. It seemed to me that they thought everything about the United States was good and everything about Poland was bad. In the eyes of the Polish people, the United States had clearly won the ideological war between capitalism and communism. However, in my efforts to assure this family that the streets of America were not in fact paved with gold, I was searching for the Polish word for "corruption." I could not remember it, so I said to the husband, "What do you call it when people in government are not honest, when they take bribes and use their political position for their own personal benefit?" He looked at me with a perfectly straight face and, believing he had found the answer to my question, said, "Communism." I burst into a fit of uncontrollable laughter, which only seemed to embarrass the man's wife and daughter. They immediately told him he should not say such things "publicly," to which the man replied, "Why not? It's true, isn't it?" It became immediately clear to me that for this man and his family, the Communist party had very little legitimacy.

This is the Poland that Lech Walesa grew up in as a young boy and worked in as a young man. He was two years old when Stalin's version of socialism first came to Poland in 1945.

CHAPTER 3

POSTWAR STRUGGLES

Lenin . . . got it wrong when he claimed "those who do not work do not eat"; Poland has reached a higher stage: here "those who do not strike do not eat meat."[1]

DANIEL SINGER

The strike led by Lech Walesa at a Gdansk shipyard in August 1980 was by no means the first example of social unrest to occur in postwar socialist Poland. Unsuccessful social upheavals in 1956, 1968, 1970, and 1976 had paved the way for the success of the 1980 strikes. Not all of these uprisings were initiated by factory workers, however. In 1968 students and intellectuals dominated the social unrest. Several factors—the Polish dissident movement, student unrest at the universities, the role of the Catholic church, and the widespread dissatisfaction of the peasants—soon overlapped and interacted with the workers' protest movement.

When looking at these events through the prism of historical perspective, one fact becomes clear: these were not isolated instances of rebellion, nor were they random protests that occurred when things got particularly bad.

Rather, they were seen as a gradual but clearly emerging pattern of popular discontent brought about by the failed political and economic policies of a socialist government forced on Poland by Russian Communists. Social dissatisfaction, especially with the economic conditions of everyday life, rose like an incoming tide, and the people held the government directly responsible for the shortcomings of the system.

The fight was between the industrial workers and the Communist party leadership. Working people were directly challenging the economic policies of the party. From a Marxist or socialist perspective, these two groups should have been one and the same. The party was, after all, supposed to be the representative of the working class, the "vanguard of the proletariat." Worker rebellions were very powerful statements that the party was not representing the workers' interests at all, but was in fact their main political enemy. Any worker unrest against the policies of the government was very embarrassing to the Communist party, both at home and abroad, and could not be tolerated by the party leaders.

Although not one of the attempts at social protest achieved all of its aims, some did achieve more than others. And even when the uprisings failed to achieve their immediate goals, there remained certain positive signs for the future of the protest movement. Each struggle was a learning process. Each brought home clear lessons to the protest leaders, whether they were dissident intellectuals or striking factory workers. They learned from their mistakes. They understood what they had done wrong. They became aware of what limits they could test, and they learned how to avoid tactical errors that might end in unnecessary bloodshed. The Gdansk shipyard strike of 1970 was a particularly important event that shaped the mind of young Lech Walesa, who saw his fellow workers mowed down by police guns. Walesa assured his fellow striking workers in 1980 that they would not make the same mistakes they'd made in 1970.[2]

The Solidarity victory of 1980 was a part of the long continuity of social protest in postwar Poland; it was the culmination of a whole series of confrontations with the Soviet-sponsored Communist government.

Another interesting feature of postwar social unrest in Poland is that these events seemed to follow a pattern. According to Neal Ascherson, a noted writer on Polish affairs, social upheavals in Poland seemed to come almost in regularly predictable cycles lasting approximately ten to fourteen years. Gdansk 1980 was one more in a series of such cycles, even if it was much more successful than any of the previous ones. Here is how the cycle generally looked:

> The cycle begins with the arrival of a new party leadership, promising more democracy, economic changes which will bring benefit directly to every Polish family. . . . Gradually the new authorities drift off course. Power becomes the monopoly of a clique out of touch with the needs and hopes of the Polish people. The economy begins to forget the consumer and wastes itself in grandiose, often futile investment projects. The industrial workers . . . see their living standards fall and their rights trampled upon until they can take no more: they rebel and the governing clique collapses. A new team arrives, once again promising a free press, respect for human rights and sausage for all, and the next cycle begins.[3]

THE UPHEAVALS OF 1956

A speech given by Nikita Khrushchev on the night of February 24, 1956, at the twentieth Soviet Party Congress in Moscow resounded throughout East Central Europe. In this so-called Secret Speech, which did not remain a secret for very long, Khrushchev delivered a stunning attack upon Stalin, who had died three years earlier. He accused Stalin of having been a brutal dictator who murdered thousands of loyal Communists. This speech marked the beginning of the de-Stalinization period in the Soviet Union and its satellite states in East Central Europe. The brutal terror and extremism of the Stalinist period had finally come to an end.

A period of political "thaw" followed Khrushchev's speech. In the next few months the people of the Soviet bloc countries began to understand that reform was now possible. A new spirit emerged, one filled with optimism and hope for a better life after Stalin. Along with it came a greater willingness to protest the shortcomings of the system. This was seen most clearly in Poland and Hungary. In Poland it led to the strikes and worker riots of June 1956.

The workers at the Zipso engineering plant in Poznan laid down their tools and marched into the center of the city in protest against the state's economic policies. They were protesting high food prices, low wages, the shortage of consumer articles, and poor working conditions. They marched down the street carrying hastily drawn banners that read, "Bread and Freedom." As they marched, they sang the national anthem and were soon joined by thousands of other residents of Poznan. Writer Flora Lewis described the scene: " 'Out with the Russians!' they cried as they pushed along. 'Down with the government!' 'We want bread and freedom!' 'Give us back our religion!' Bursting lungs roared out everything that for twelve years could not be whispered. 'Free the prisoners!' 'Down with the U.B. [the Polish secret police].' "[4]

The crowd soon turned into a mob. The demonstrators attacked police and prison headquarters, threw archival material and secret files out the windows, and set the papers on fire in the street. Polish authorities reacted by turning the police force loose on the demonstrators. Prime Minister Józef Cyrankiewicz said the uprising was a capitalist plot inspired by antisocialist counterrevolutionaries. He further proclaimed, "Every provocateur or madman who dares to lift his hand against the power of People's [Socialist] Poland will have that hand chopped off."[5] Nearly sixty people were killed and over two hundred were wounded. Hundreds of others were arrested. (At the time, Lech Walesa was a twelve-year-old schoolboy living less than one hundred fifty miles away.)

The strike in Poznan came to an abrupt end, a dismal failure for the Poznan workers. The workers had no leaders, no plan or strategy, no organization or communications network, and no weapons with which to fight the government. But this first significant worker protest in postwar Poland had left the Communist leaders with many unanswered questions: Why were the workers so unhappy? How was it possible that they were so much at odds with the Communist party that claimed to represent them? Wasn't the party supposed to be the vanguard of the proletariat? These same questions would be asked again and again over the next few decades. And they would be asked again most strongly in December of 1980 while the eyes of the world were on Lech Walesa.

The political thaw that followed Khrushchev's speech and the political embarrassment over the Zipso incident both contributed to the change in leadership that took place in Poland in the fall of 1956. But this change did not come about without a fight. Wladyslaw Gomulka was reinstated as first secretary of the Communist party. Gomulka, a loyal Communist, had lost his position as party chief during a Stalinist purge in 1948. He had been accused of trying to formulate his own "Polish path to socialism" instead of automatically adopting the Soviet model of development. He had even been arrested in 1951 and had spent nearly three years in jail. Stalin had been particularly upset with his open refusal to collectivize agriculture. Gomulka's Polish way to socialism had antagonized Moscow, but had endeared him to the Poles, who saw him standing up to the Russians. They supported his return to power in the fall of 1956.

The leaders in Moscow, including Khrushchev himself, were not overjoyed at the prospect of Gomulka's return. Despite the Soviets' open opposition, Poland's Communist party was on the verge of electing Gomulka party chief. For a while the situation was extremely tense. Khrushchev and his henchmen, including Foreign Minister Vyacheslav Molotov, flew to Warsaw to make sure Gomulka would not return to power. Soviet troops were mobilized, and Soviet tanks were poised to move on Warsaw at a moment's notice. The nation was on the brink of war. After heated negotiations that lasted nearly all night, Khrushchev reluctantly agreed to allow Gomulka to return to office. He was not the man Moscow preferred, but at least he was a loyal Communist. The entire event was a sharp departure from the arbitrariness and inflexibility of the Stalinist era.

In Poland, Gomulka was greeted as a national hero. He had stood up to the Russians and won. His popularity was now widespread throughout Poland, and his government in 1956 did possess some measure of legitimacy. People saw in him an expression of Polish nationalism, the spirit of the struggling Pole resisting foreign intervention. In a speech to the nation delivered just before he was sworn in as first secretary, Gomulka attacked the memory of Stalin, denounced the economic policies of the last years, and even praised the Poznan workers who had so vehemently protested those policies.

Gomulka's return to power in 1956 marked the end of the Stalinist period of Polish history. Hundreds of people were released from prison. People were allowed to travel abroad much more freely. Western art and music were no longer taboo. Repression of religion was eased. Cardinal Wyszynski, who had spent most of the Stalinist period in prison, was quickly released, signaling that perhaps a new relationship between the government and the Catholic church was now possible. Many other rigid policies were revised. As Daniel Singer has written, "People began to speak up and even to write in an entirely different manner, though the censorship was never lifted."[6] This new spirit that began to develop in Poland in the fall of 1956 is sometimes referred to as the Spring in October, or simply the Polish October.

In Hungary, however, the new spirit of reform after de-Stalinization led to a very different outcome. The Hungarians had watched events unfurl in Poland closely and hoped for a similar success story. But they were less willing to compromise than the Poles, and they demanded a more Western system. Eventually the reformist spirit led to a full-fledged Hungarian uprising against Soviet-style Communist policies. Khrushchev would not back down a second time. On November 4, 1956, Soviet tanks rolled in and crushed the Hungarian revolt. At the time there was much Polish support for the

Hungarian cause. Although many Poles were ready to bring Poland directly into the armed struggle on the side of Hungary, cooler heads prevailed. Among them was Cardinal Wyszynski, who in an emotional speech to the nation saved Poland from much bloodshed by asking the Poles to act with moderation.

The events of October in Poland had shown once again that Poland was still fighting for independence, if only in a very limited way. This nationalistic struggle for a specifically Polish way to socialism is important. For one thing, it set a precedent that was later to reappear in the form of the Solidarity movement in 1980. Beginning with Gomulka, Poland was able to go its own way—not completely, of course, but just enough to preserve a sense of the uniqueness of the Polish situation. For example, Gomulka allowed the collective farms, which had been set up by force during the Six-Year Plan of 1950 to 1955, to disband. The peasants took back their land with shouts of joyous enthusiasm even before the official orders came through. But the absence of collective agriculture was a clear departure from the Soviet model of socialism. Polish nationalism and tradition played the key role in Gomulka's logic. His decision was not antisocialist by any means. He simply felt that the uniqueness and tradition of Polish culture would not yet allow the implementation of socialist agricultural policies. Poland would have to go more slowly and find its own path to socialism.

Despite a promising beginning, Gomulka did not remain popular for very long. It soon became clear to the people that his policies would not bring political democratization. He refused to let worker councils have any real power, preferring instead to allow the Communist party to retain the power monopoly. Nor did his economic policies soon bring economic prosperity and a better material life. Every year the people heard the same story: They would have to defer the better life while Poland was in the process of industrializing. The surplus wealth of the nation had to go into heavy industry, not consumer goods. Only later would the people be rewarded for their patience, and the material well-being of the whole society would follow. But the good life never came; the people had only more empty promises.

Disillusionment with Gomulka's economic and political policies had grown more pronounced by the early 1960s. Some former Marxist sympathizers and other intellectuals turned against the hypocrisy of the Communist party and began to openly criticize the government. These people became known as dissidents because they disagreed with official state policy. Two such radical dissidents, Jacek Kuron (later of Solidarity fame) and Karol Modzelewski, went so far as to write an open letter to the Communist party in 1964. They attacked Gomulka for his nondemocratic programs and for allowing the ruling Communist bureaucracy to exploit the working people. They were both arrested and sentenced to three and a half years in prison, but they vowed to continue their criticism of the Communist party. The open letter marked a new beginning for the dissident movement in postwar Poland. A small core of dedicated intellectuals decided that political repression and brutality would not keep them from criticizing the actions of the government. Some of these radical dissidents were Jewish, and in 1968 this would have severe consequences for them.

MARCH 1968

In March of 1968 university students and intellectuals rose up in protest against the increasingly restrictive cultural policies of the government. They were particularly upset with government censorship. These were not factory workers striking over such bread-and-butter issues as prices and wages, but rather intellectuals staging social protests over the question of freedom of speech. Poles joked sarcastically that the commandment for intellectuals went like this: "Above all don't think. And if you must think, don't speak. And if you must speak, don't write. But if you must write, don't sign it. And if you must sign it, make sure it's only *self*-criticism."

The specific incident that touched off the crisis was the closing by the government of a nationalistic play in Warsaw.

The play was called *The Forefathers* (*Dziady*), and it was written in the early nineteenth century by one of Poland's most famous writers, Adam Mickiewicz. Among other things, it dealt with the issue of Russian tyranny at the time of the partitions, when Poland was under Russian domination and fighting to regain its independence. Specifically, it recounted the story of the Polish struggle for freedom in the November uprising of 1830.

Audiences attending the play rose to their feet and broke out in long, boisterous applause every time an anti-Russian line was delivered in the play. It was as if "a bomb went off," said Gustaw Holoubek, the actor who played the leading role in the play. These strong anti-Russian feelings, generated by a deep sense of Polish patriotism, were too much for the government to ignore. Anti-Russian sentiment and Polish nationalism had been powerful forces in Poland's history. This could only add to popular sentiment against the legitimacy of the Soviet-dominated Communist party of Poland. Even though the play told of the struggle against the tyranny of the Russian czar, and not the struggle against Soviet communism, the parallels were still too close to home. The play was shut down by the Polish authorities on January 30, 1968.

Here is an account by a Polish dissident who attended the last performance of the play:

> The air was electric. We knew the play, one of the masterpieces of our dramatic tradition, was being closed that night on Gomulka's orders. There were small demonstrations at every nationalist line [in the play]. At the end, the applause lasted more than half an hour. We then all sang the national anthem "Jeszcze Polska Nie Zginela" (Poland Has Not Yet Perished) over and over and over. . . . We marched to the Mickiewicz monument on Krakowskie Przedmiescie, where the police were ready with their riot gear. There was no large riot, but the police were particularly brutal and arrested a few dozen demonstrators.[7]

The intellectual community of Poland, especially the students and faculty at Warsaw University, strongly objected to the closing of the play. By March, demonstrations against the censorship of artistic expression were being organized by student organizations in Warsaw. General Mieczyslaw Moczar, minister of the interior and therefore head of the dreaded security police, reacted by bringing in thugs and "angry workers" to attack the students. The riots that followed became an excuse for the security police to arrest the demonstrators.

A group of Jewish university students known as the Commandos had previously circulated a petition protesting the closing of the play.[8] Moczar, already known for his blatant anti-Semitism, used this incident to start a renewed campaign against Jews in Poland, whether they were part of the protest movement or not. People of Jewish origin were routinely dismissed from the Party, from the universities, and from responsible positions.[9] While Moczar preferred to blame the Jews for starting the disturbances, the government attacked other groups as well, including non-Jewish dissident faculty members from the universities, and student "troublemakers." Political opponents who did not toe the Party line were also conveniently dismissed from their posts. Later that same year (1968) thousands of Jews left Poland to escape political persecution and Polish anti-Semitism. Moczar's manipulations succeeded in purging Poland of most of its remaining Jews. The affair was a sad, embarrassing chapter in Polish history.

While the protests of March 1968 were winding down in Poland, the Prague Spring in Czechoslovakia was just beginning. A new Communist party chief, Alexander Dubček, began to introduce liberal reform policies in Czechoslovakia in the spring of 1968. Because these reforms promised a gradual democratization of society, they were unacceptable to Brezhnev, the Soviet leader, and he pressured Dubček to end them. Dubček defiantly refused to back down, and this prompted a Soviet military invasion of Czechoslovakia. Dozens of Czechs were killed. In 1969 Dubček's government was replaced by a pro-Soviet puppet regime. All of Poland, including twenty-five-year-old Lech Walesa, learned that any emerging democratic movement in East Central Europe was at the mercy of Soviet tanks. Ironically, Polish troops were used as part of the invasion force, as Gomulka wanted to prove his loyalty to Brezhnev.

One of the main reasons for the failure of the protests in Poland in 1968 was that the urban factory workers did not join in and ally themselves with the intellectuals. As a result, there was a gulf between the workers and the intellectuals which prevented any coordinated action. As one writer put it, "One could argue that March 1968 represented the deepest chasm between two crucial strata of Polish society, a gap that was not bridged for the next eight years."[10]

The students and intellectuals, in turn, did not take part in the events of December 1970 when the workers on the Baltic coast rose up in protest against the price hikes of the Gomulka regime. Instead, the intellectuals remained passive. This gulf between the workers and the intellectuals represented a very serious obstacle to the success of any protest movement in Poland. The absence of coordinated action[11] among various dissatisfied elements of Polish society kept the opposition divided and served the purposes of the Communist regime. The gap between workers and intellectuals was not closed until after the factory riots of 1976 when a Committee for Defense of Workers (known as KOR, Komitet Obrony Robotników) was founded by intellectuals to support strike leaders and workers who had been arrested for their part in the riots.

1970 STRIKE

The events of December 1970 were centered in the Baltic seaports of Gdansk, Gdynia, and Szczecin. Shipyard workers in these cities became the focus of a massive series of strikes. About fifty thousand workers were employed there in the numerous shipyards and in related industries. (In the Lenin shipyards of Gdansk, Lech Walesa was then a twenty-seven-year-old worker.)

The pattern of the unrest that took place in December once again fit the established cycle of social upheavals. It started with worker dissatisfaction with proposed changes in wages that would have lowered their purchasing power. To this was added substantial price changes on many consumer items. This was announced to the nation on December 12, just two weeks before Christmas. Some prices, like those of television sets, were slightly lowered, but most prices, especially for food, were increased by 10 to 20 percent. The workers at the Lenin shipyards reacted in a spontaneous burst of protest. A strike declaration was followed by street violence, confusion, and panic. The authorities declared a state of emergency. The entire incident lasted five days. When it was over, dozens of people were dead, and many more were wounded. (The exact number of dead is not known, even to this day.) All the major Baltic ports of Poland were soon teeming with social unrest. Workers in Gdynia at the Paris Commune shipyard and in Szczecin at the Warski shipyard had found out about the strikes, and they started their own strikes in sympathy with their Gdansk colleagues.

Soon after the strikes began, the workers left the Lenin shipyard and marched on the local Communist party headquarters in Gdansk. As they walked along the streets, they sang patriotic and religious songs. They were quickly joined by enthusiastic crowds who were only too happy to join in a protest against the latest government price increases. A strike committee had developed an eleven-point platform. It included numerous economic demands, guarantees that the strikers would not be punished for starting the strike, and a call for more political democratization of the country. But there was really no organized or rationally thought-out strategy for dealing with the government, no coordinated or systematic plan of action by the strike leaders to achieve their goals. They simply presented their demands to the Communist party leadership and waited for a response. In the meantime, however, they could not control the spontaneous street demonstrations. In 1980, Lech Walesa was to remark: "Do you know what our biggest error was [in 1970]? We had no leader, no one who could play the role that I have assumed in the present strike. In my subconscious I was waiting then for some charismatic leader to appear. I was young, stubborn, single-minded, but I was no leader. Had I known in 1970 what I know now, history might have run a little differently."[12]

Wild rumors spread quickly, many of them untrue. For example, it was said that the police troops were actually Russians in Polish uniforms. Panic and fear replaced logic and reason. The crowd soon turned violent, and confrontations with the security forces became more frequent. Angry workers set the Communist party headquarters on fire. The regime reacted by giving the police orders to shoot.

Lech Walesa had been working at the Gdansk shipyard for about three years when this strike occurred. He was actively involved in the strike and served on one of the strike committees. He lived through the folly of the street methods of the strikers. In 1980 Walesa reflected on these events in an interview with a German journalist:

> At that time I was only out on the street once. I sat in the Lenin shipyard on the strike committee. Only I was too young and too dumb. That it came to such riots here in Gdansk, that was our mistake. Many of my colleagues say that I don't have the right to say such a thing. But I was there in 1970, and I know how it was. I could not have prevented what happened. But I am not one of those who believe that shots were fired here in Gdansk without any reason. In reality the police had no other way out.[13]

Although the errors of those strikers were many, they could all be reduced to one major flaw. The striking workers failed to comprehend this at the time, but Walesa would understand it well in 1980: any hope of success would require a political solution to the confrontation, and this solution could not be found through the use of violence or street demonstrations. Serious negotiations with the government were required. The workers had to use their strike as a weapon to force the regime to talk with them, not fight with them.

This philosophy was wise political strategy, and justifiable from a moral standpoint. The Catholic church could not approve of violent confrontations with the government, but it could lend its support wholeheartedly to worker demands for peaceful negotiations. Not insignificantly, this insistence on nonviolence was also one of the main reasons Walesa was awarded the Nobel Peace Prize in 1983.

Not only was nonviolence the best policy; it represented the workers' only hope of real success. Violence meant direct confrontation with the government, making negotiation and compromise impossible. Backing down at that point would have meant a loss of face. The government could not hope to rule the country effectively if it allowed workers to take to the streets in violent protest.

Unfortunately, in 1970 violence won out over negotiations. The legitimacy of the Gomulka regime, or what was left of it, was totally shattered in the process. Polish workers had risen up against the man who headed the political party claiming to represent them. The myth of the workers' state had been directly challenged, and the situation was embarrassing politically. Even Moscow hinted in a letter to the Communist party of Poland that perhaps it was time for Gomulka to go. On December 20, 1970, Edward Gierek replaced him as first secretary of the Communist party in Poland.

Gierek, who himself was once a coal miner in Silesia, appealed directly to the workers: "Trust me. I was once one of you, an ordinary laborer. I am on your side." Later he even appeared personally at the Lenin shipyard, where he gave a very emotional speech urging the workers to give him a chance by supporting his policies. "Help me to help you," he told them in a statement that would soon become famous. The workers responded favorably and with equal emotion. "Yes, we will help you," they cried back in response, and they agreed to go back to work. Walesa was one of those people who believed that Gierek should be given a chance to prove himself. Anna Walentynowicz, who was to play a major role as a strike leader in Solidarity in 1980, was another worker at the shipyards who, with tears in her eyes, listened to Gierek's emotional plea for help.

The final decision by the government to reverse its price increases was reached only after the textile factory strikes in Lodz in February of 1971. A few weeks after the Baltic coast strikes had been settled, workers in the textile factories of Lodz, Poland's second largest city, went on strike. Gierek sent the new premier of Poland, Piotr Jaroszewicz, to meet with groups of hostile women workers from these factories. The women flatly refused the premier's plea for help until prices were lowered or wages were increased. It was too dangerous at that time for the government to risk direct confrontation with the women of Poland. All of Poland might have been up in arms if Poland's mothers, wives, and daughters were found lying dead in the streets in a repeat of the Baltic coast violence. In a sudden reversal, the government announced a complete price rollback to the original levels in effect before the increases of December 12.

The Baltic coast strikes of December 1970 should not be seen as just another in a series of strikes in the history of worker unrest in postwar Poland. They were a major precedent-setting event. First of all, the strikes had a profound impact on the relationship between the government and the workers. Although the strikers failed to achieve their specific goals, their actions did bring down the government. Wladyslaw Gomulka was forced to resign as first secretary of the Communist party. Although this change in leadership did not change the fundamental structure of power in the country, it was still a very significant political development. As Daniel Singer has written, "Never before in the history of the Soviet bloc did workers, fighting on their own, topple the party leadership and bring down the government."[14] In the future, any new government would be extremely fearful of antagonizing the workers and thus prompting them to go on strike again. Despite their apparent failure, the strikes did leave the workers with a real sense of their own power when they acted in a united way.

The strikes of 1970 also affected the entire economic system of Poland. Because of the fear of future social unrest, the new government kept the prices of staple food articles such as meat, butter, bread, and dairy products artificially low so as not to antagonize the workers. This changed governmental economic policy in a way that ultimately strapped Polish socialism into an economic bind from which it could not escape. Specifically, it meant that the government had to pay huge subsidies to support prices that were well below the market rate. This in turn led directly to contradictory and irrational economic decisions as well as more severe food shortages. In accordance with the law of supply and demand, which did not cease to operate simply because Poland was a socialist system, artificially low prices meant that nearly everyone could afford the goods. The real problem became finding enough goods to buy.

This led to an absurd economic situation: it cost more to produce certain goods than the prices for which they were selling. Since the production of such goods had to be operated at a loss, there was no real incentive to produce them. Economically, it made no sense at all, and the government economists knew it. It was done for purely political reasons. No capitalist business could have survived such a situation for very long. But Poland had a socialist economy. It could and did survive the immediate future, but only at a tremendous long-term economic cost.

Finally, the strikes of 1970 contributed to the crisis of legitimacy. As we have seen, there had already been a serious legitimacy problem for the government in postwar Poland. When the authorities resorted to the use of violence, the problem was intensified. Poles had killed Poles. The whole society, not just the factory workers in Gdansk, were further alienated from the Communist party. Increasingly, the government's power became based upon military force, backed up by the Soviet army, and not upon any real trust on the part of the people. This immense popular dissatisfaction only needed a way to manifest itself. This is exactly what happened in 1980 in the Solidarity trade union.

Despite the powerful impact of the events of 1970 on the future of social unrest in Poland, the December strikes were seen at the time as a terrible personal tragedy for all involved; they were also viewed as a dismal political failure. Walesa, as one of the strike activists in 1970, is still haunted by the memory of those tragic days: "December 1970 was my greatest defeat. . . . We had a chance, but I was twenty-seven years old and I had no experience. Over ten years I've had a lot of time to rethink everything, to analyze every detail. The spilled blood would not let me forget."[15]

THE EVENTS OF 1975 TO 1976

In the mid-1970s the important issue of human rights surfaced in the international arena. In the summer of 1975 representatives of the nations of the world met in Helsinki, Finland, to discuss this issue. On August 1, 1975, they reached an agreement on human rights violations that came to be known as the Helsinki Accords. Thirty-five nations, including Poland, signed the accords. The clauses of the agreements guaranteed "fundamental freedoms, including freedom of thought, conscience, religion, and belief." These human rights clauses were referred to again and again in Poland. Dissidents and intellectuals were poised and ready to point out any violations in Poland. Later, American president Jimmy Carter's foreign policy also focused on the question of human rights violations, and this added moral support to the Polish cause.

Another important development was the creation of "flying universities," which were set up after the 1976 strikes. They were called flying universities because groups met for secret lectures in people's homes, changing locations frequently to avoid detection by the state's internal security force. Professors caught giving such lectures were harassed and punished by the police. Forbidden lectures were given about the true history of Poland, free from the distortions of the Communist version. Students and faculty now freely discussed the truth, as opposed to the censored version of history that the state had provided. Students joked that in their required Communist-theory classes they highlighted the most important material with black Magic Markers.

Protests by the academic and intellectual community of Poland occurred in 1975 and 1976. After a routine visit to Poland by Brezhnev, head of the Communist party in the Soviet Union, changes in the Polish constitution were proposed. Clauses were to be added that asserted the leading role of the Communist party in Polish life and the permanence of the political alliance with the Soviet Union, known as the Warsaw Pact. (Both of these issues were later to become major sticking points in the Gdansk agreements signed by Lech Walesa in 1980.) The widespread and unexpected social outrage at the proposed changes in the Polish constitution led the Party to drop the issue entirely.

In June of 1976 the government once again felt it was time to address some of the major economic problems of the country. In an attempt to bring the cost of producing goods in line with their prices, it announced major price increases. Some meat and dairy prices were increased by over 50 percent. Disgruntled workers throughout Poland reacted by laying down their tools and walking off their jobs. At first it seemed as if it might be a repeat of the events of 1970. However, the government's appeals for more sacrifices on the part of the workers did not make an impression this time. They had heard that story too many times in the past. They had become much too alienated politically, and they no longer believed the government's promises.

The price hikes of June 1976 seemed to be a catalyst for the venting of the enormous anger the workers were feeling. The first physical outbursts of pent-up worker frustration occurred in the Ursus tractor factory just outside Warsaw and in the industrial city of Radom, located to the south of Warsaw. In Radom, workers from the General Walter armament works left their stations and marched on the local Party headquarters, singing revolutionary and religious songs. They were enthusiastically greeted by thousands of Radom residents and workers from other factories. As in Gdansk in 1970, the crowd soon turned into an angry mob. They stormed and looted the Communist party headquarters and found that luxury items unavailable to the common person had been hidden in the building, specially set aside for the privileged Party members. The workers jubilantly passed these goods to the cheering crowds waiting outside. But the police soon got the upper hand and dispersed the crowds, arresting and injuring many in the process.

Meanwhile, at the Ursus factory, striking workers became violent. They stormed out of the factory and proceeded to block the railroad tracks. This action was a reflection of a very sensitive issue among Polish citizens. Right or wrong, many Polish citizens believed that one of the main reasons Poland did not have enough goods was that they were being sent to the Soviet Union, a result of trade agreements not beneficial to Poland. Blocking the rail lines out of the country was, therefore, a very radical action. It was symbolic of the general desire for political freedom from Soviet influence.

Strike fever spread like wildfire throughout Poland. Before the government could fully respond to the Radom and Ursus incidents, strikes broke out in other cities, including Plock, Gdansk, Poznan, and Lodz. It soon became clear that the government had once again miscalculated the mood of the nation. In the face of massive social protest, the government was forced to back down again. Piotr Jaroszewicz, premier of Poland and a prominent figure in the Communist party, appeared on state-controlled television and radio to announce that all price increases would be canceled, effective immediately. The crisis ended before the next day was over; the strikers went back to work. It was a humiliating defeat for the government, and a very embarrassing moment for Jaroszewicz personally.

The incompetence of the regime became increasingly apparent to most Poles. First, without any warning or public consultation, the leaders of the government declared major price hikes. Then, just as suddenly, they rescinded them. It seemed to many that the government really did not know what it was doing. It was akin to members of the American Congress passing major pay raises for themselves in the middle of the night when no one would see what they were doing, then canceling their raises in the light of day when people found out and reacted in anger. A famous Polish comedian, dancer, and singer, Andrzej Rosiewicz, reflected the mood of the nation when he made fun of premier Jaroszewicz as part of his routine in nightclubs and cabarets. "Who is the stupidest man in all of Poland?" Rosiewicz asked his audiences. "I, Rosiewicz, am," he told them. But in Polish, the word for "I" is "Ja." Placed before the comic's last name, Rosiewicz, this was the exact pronunciation of the premier's name: "Jarosiewicz." This play on words did not amuse the authorities, who quickly closed down Rosiewicz's act. But Poles everywhere talked about the incident for weeks. Rosiewicz became an instant hero among his countrymen, a new symbol of resistance to government folly.

As with the earlier strikes, the results of the crisis of June 1976 were important in paving the way for the ultimate success of the 1980 Solidarity strikes led by Lech Walesa. First, the events of June 1976 forced the government to make major economic concessions. It backed down and reversed its price hikes. In a sense, the workers had vetoed the government's decisions; they had said no, and the government had quickly reversed its economic policy. It now seemed to the workers that they had some sort of direct veto power over government policies. Although their actions did not bring down the government, they very well could have if the government had not backed down so quickly. Even so, the workers had succeeded in dramatically affecting economic policy, and their own sense of power grew as a result.

Second, the events of June 1976 also helped forge ties between workers and intellectuals. Although the price hikes were reversed, many people who had been arrested during the riots remained in jail. To defend their legal rights the imprisoned workers needed lawyers. Also, their families would need financial support during the time of their imprisonment. Adam Michnik and Jacek Kuron, two longtime radical dissidents, worked to set up an organization to defend the rights of these workers. A Committee for Defense of Workers (known as KOR) was formed after the 1976 strikes, and it had considerable success in protecting the arrested workers.

The creation of KOR (which later changed its name officially to KSS, the Committee for Social Self-Defense) marked a significant turning point in the history of Poland's protest movement. The basis for a worker-intellectual alliance now existed, and it proved to be a much more formidable foe for the government than either group acting alone. Lech Walesa would skillfully use this alliance four years later during the strikes in Gdansk.

THE POPE'S VISIT IN 1979

A real turning point in church-state relations in Poland came in October 1978 with the election of Polish-born Karol Wojtyla, cardinal of Cracow, as pope. The previous pope, John Paul I, had died unexpectedly after having served only a short time as head of the Roman Catholic church. Wojtyla chose the name John Paul II in his honor. The whole world was astounded by this turn of events. It was the first time in 456 years that a non-Italian had been chosen as the successor to Saint Peter in Rome. Imagine—a pope being selected from a Communist country of the Soviet bloc! This was the stuff of novels, not reality, and yet it happened.

No one in Poland was expecting such an event—not the government, not the clergy, not the common people. It came as a total shock to everyone. Many even refused to believe it at first, thinking it was a cruel hoax. When Poles finally realized it was true, they laughed, they cried for joy, and they started to celebrate. Crowds gathered spontaneously in public squares throughout Poland, singing and hugging one another in utter joy, still wondering if they would wake up from their dream and find that it was not so. An electrician in Gdansk named Lech Walesa, his wife Danuta, and their many children were among them. The government, for its part, was conspicuously silent, not knowing how to respond. It merely announced the news without comment.

More than any other single event of the 1970s, the election of Karol Wojtyla of Poland as head of the Roman Catholic church had a profound impact on Polish society. His selection had a direct influence on the hearts and minds of the Polish people. It allowed them to see that anything was possible and that things could change for the better. More than anything else, Polish society started believing in itself again. It had been given the message of hope.

The pope asked Polish authorities if he could make his first trip back to his native land as the head of the Roman Catholic church in June 1979. At first, the Communist authorities were reluctant to agree to the visit. They were perfectly aware of the danger his visit represented. The pope presented a serious challenge to their authority, not in the sense of immediate political power, but in terms of moral power, and that was perhaps just as dangerous. The people owed their first loyalty to the church, not to the Communist party. But soon, realizing that it was impossible for them to object to the pope's visit, the authorities reluctantly agreed. How could they deny a native son, a Pole who had achieved such a distinguished position, the right to return to his own country for a short visit? All of Poland would have been up in arms if the government had rejected the pope's petition.

In many ways the election of the Polish pope also paved the way for the kind of social protest and social consciousness that ultimately weakened the power of the government. The visit itself was a constant source of embarrassment to the Communist regime. In every city, crowds massed in the hundreds of thousands to hear the pope speak. Lech Walesa and his family were there too. At that time, Walesa was unknown to most Poles; he was just one of millions who had come to listen. He never dreamed then that, in less than a year, he would become nearly as famous as the pontiff.

Polish television tried to downplay the impact of the pope's visit. He was only shown close up, never with more than a few dozen people around him. Poles laughed at this obvious trick of the camera. No one believed it for a second. Everyone knew that wherever the pope went, hundreds of thousands of Poles were there to greet him. People became even more resentful of the government for trying to diminish the joy of the pope's visit.

Like the upheavals of the past, the visit of John Paul II in the summer of 1979 helped prepare the way for the later success of Lech Walesa's Solidarity movement. The pontiff's speeches inspired the Poles. His moral support of the Polish workers gave Lech Walesa and his fellow activists the strength to continue their fight against the system. It gave them the courage to believe in the moral justice of their cause. The pope often spoke of the dignity of work. He gave them this message personally during his visit in the summer of 1979, less than fifteen months before the workers of Gdansk went on strike.

Another aspect of the pope's visit that helped prepare the way for the ultimate success of Solidarity was the logistics factor—the deployment of people, equipment, and supplies. During his visit, the pope traveled to many different cities in Poland and had many different speaking engagements, all scheduled at a very hectic pace. Whole grandstands were often built to hold the audiences for his speeches, only to be torn down as soon as he left. Thousands of guards had to be organized to control the enormous crowds. All this required massive logistical organization and coordination as well as a highly developed communications network. Since the authorities had almost nothing to do with the pope's itinerary or schedule, it was left up to church organizations and volunteers. It was a vast learning experience that later proved invaluable. Many people who helped coordinate the pope's visit in 1979 were Catholic intellectuals, dissidents, and political activists. Some of them later worked for Lech Walesa and Solidarity, doing the kind of work they had learned to do during the pope's visit: coordinating, communicating, and organizing.

CHAPTER 4

WALESA'S EARLY LIFE AND POLITICAL ACTIVITY

A man of our times cannot have a clear conscience so long as . . . man's natural pursuit of freedom, a decent life and happiness are countered by violence, oppression and exploitation.[1]

LECH WALESA

Lech Walesa was born on September 29, 1943, in Popowo, Poland. He was one of seven children. His family was poor, and they lived in a two-room hut. They were rural people, and Walesa would often refer to his "peasant roots." Popowo was a poor farming village located southeast of the Baltic port of Gdansk. His great-grandfather had been a relatively large landowner, a member of the gentry, or aristocratic class. Over the years his great-grandfather's many children divided the land into many smaller farms. His children's children, in turn, divided the land among their many children, so that by the time Lech's father, Boleslaw Walesa, inherited a strip of land, it was too small to support his family. Boleslaw learned a second trade, carpentry, to supplement the income from his farm.

The land troubles of the Walesa family were by no means unique. It was a problem that plagued all of Poland in the late nineteenth and early twentieth centuries. Severe rural overpopulation led to a critical shortage of land. Industrial development had been too slow to provide enough jobs for the excess rural population. Due to this lack of outside employment for their children, the peasants were forced to divide their farms into ever smaller plots so that each child would have at least a piece of the family farm. Eventually the farms became too small to support a family.[2] This rural poverty prompted thousands of Poles to seek a better life in the Western Hemisphere and Western Europe. Most of the Polish emigrants went to America, Germany, and Argentina. Rural overpopulation remained Poland's most pressing social and economic problem right up to World War II, when the severe casualties of war mercilessly "solved" the problem.

It was during this period that Lech was born. His country was still under German occupation in 1943, and the war against Hitler would last another two years. Boleslaw Walesa was sent to a German labor camp toward the end of World War II. He died soon after the war ended, sick and weak, exhausted from the hardships he had endured at the camp, which included frequent beatings and sleeping in the bitter cold. Lech was three years old at the time and never got to know him. His mother later married her husband's younger brother, Stanislaw Walesa.

In school, Lech was considered a very stubborn but courageous boy. Once he made up his mind, there was no getting him to change it. Lech was not a model student by any means; he preferred to work with his hands. He especially enjoyed tinkering with mechanical devices. In school he got mostly C's and D's, and more than one F in history. In his autobiography, he wrote: "History, it has to be said, was my weak point. One year I really landed myself in trouble when I received three failures at the end of the term. I didn't appreciate the value of history until much later. As a subject, it seemed to me remote from real life, an abstraction, describing people and facts devoid of the slightest link to reality as I knew it."[3]

Walesa is also remembered as a rowdy youth. He received a number of warnings for misbehavior, including three for smoking cigarettes in the dormitory. During the Gdansk strikes, Walesa would become famous for his chain-smoking, a habit he finally managed to break only recently.

As a child, Lech's mother read to him from the works of Polish nationalist authors, and as an adult he modeled himself after Józef Piłsudski, a marshal in the Polish army who became famous for his victory over the Russians in the Polish-Soviet War of 1919–1920. The victory became known as the Miracle on the Vistula and is still widely celebrated by Poles as an important victory over the Russian invaders. It also kept Lenin's communism from moving westward. Piłsudski was a rather authoritarian figure who later seized power in Poland in a government coup in 1926. Lech's grandfather, Jan, claimed to have known Piłsudski personally and said he even helped Piłsudski escape from his enemies once by disguising him in women's clothing. Many thought Jan had just made up the story.

Walesa quickly became impatient with stuffy scholarly inquiry and literary studies. His mind was always racing to a new topic. He once boasted that he had never completely finished reading a book, because he always got bored and went on to a different subject. Lech was the first member of his family to be educated. But instead of going to a university, he went to a vocational school in Lipno, where he learned the electrical trade. He graduated in 1961 at eighteen and took a job at an agricultural cooperative (a type of collective farm) in Lochocino, a neighboring village, repairing electrical machines. He was very skilled at his trade, and his intense curiosity would cause him to take apart complex electrical parts and put them back together again just to see what made them tick.

Walesa served two years in the army, from 1963 to 1965, ending his service with the rank of corporal. According to the official military records, his file rather prophetically included mention of his "enormous leadership instinct." He was described as a "natural-born commander" capable of making "flash decisions."[4] Walesa was already showing some of the charisma that would one day make him famous.

Lech was raised as a devout Roman Catholic; his family had an outdoor statue of the Virgin Mary before which they prayed. Although he did receive a strong foundation in Catholicism, as a teenager he went through a brief period of religious neglect. Later, as a young adult, he rediscovered his religious leanings. Here is how he described the turning point of his religious life: "One day I felt very cold, very tired, and I started looking for a place to rest. There was nothing around but a church. So I entered the church and sat down on a bench. And I immediately got well."[5] Later, through the church, Walesa met Polish intellectual dissidents in KOR.

When he moved to Gdansk in May 1967, Walesa went to work as a shipyard electrician at the Lenin shipyard. He was just one of thousands of workers at the shipyard, a fact that made him feel like a "tiny cog in a vast machine." His first job was to lay cables on large factory-fishing boats, dividing the cable into sections, then separating and stripping all the wires. He did not particularly like the specialized nature of the work, as he preferred to be a jack-of-all-trades. "I realized that I couldn't use many of the skills I knew by heart from earlier jobs. To be a specialist worker, with one small task, never appealed to me."[6]

Two years later he met his future wife, Miroslawa Danuta Golos. It was love at first sight:

> One day I passed by a flower stand and caught sight of a pair of mischievous brown eyes in a sweet face framed by long dark hair; it was a vision I couldn't get out of my mind. A few days later I went back to ask her what time she got off work. She told me she lived with her aunt in the suburbs . . . and, like me, had arrived in Gdansk from a

> country village. . . . I preferred her middle name, Danuta, or Danka, as I soon began calling her.[7]

They were married in November 1969, only two months after they had met. Apartments in Gdansk were so hard to come by and so expensive that the newly married Walesas were forced to rent tiny rooms, which they sometimes had to share with other people: "We started married life poor as church mice. There was no question of going back to my bachelor's quarters, so with virtually no money, we began our years of wandering, from one inhospitable rented room to the next, leaving a bit of ourselves behind each time we moved on. We finally found a place to our liking on Beethoven Street, an attic over a hairdresser's salon."[8]

A large family was part of Lech's family tradition, and he and Danuta soon had the first of their eight children. Danuta became a great source of emotional strength for Lech. Her moral support remained firm despite all the economic hardships the family faced.

Walesa's political activism began soon after he started working at the shipyard, and he quickly earned a reputation as a political troublemaker. At the time of the Gdansk strikes of 1970 (see Chapter 3), Walesa, at twenty-seven, had already been one of the strike leaders. Because of his activism Walesa was frequently harassed by the security police. He was constantly shadowed and interrogated, so that his life became a continual cat-and-mouse game with the police. According to a Polish detention law, people held by the police had to be formally charged with a crime within forty-eight hours or else they had to be released. One method of harassment was to arrest people, hold them just under the forty-eight-hour time limit, and then release them. Walesa was detained by the police in this fashion so many times that he no longer remembers the exact number. Since he took great pains not to break the law in any other way, the police were never able to officially charge him with a crime.

In 1971 Walesa was selected in the local trade union elections as an inspector of working conditions. Writer Robert Eringer interviewed Walesa's friend and fellow activist, who reflected on that position:

> "This function suited him most," recalls Lenarciak. "He wanted to understand the mood of the whole shipyard and as a union inspector he had the right to walk anywhere and talk to anyone. . . . " It was a wise position to take. Walesa was able to spread himself out and gain popularity in all corners of the shipyard.[9]

During this period Walesa became disillusioned with the local trade union's lack of any real authority. It became increasingly clear to him that the trade union's power was mythical. Real power rested with management and, by extension, with the Communist party leadership. The workers' union had no real authority to defend the rights of the workers. The next year, burdened by problems at home, he withdrew from the union elections. But at this time he learned an important lesson that he would not forget in 1980: The creation of free and independent trade unions was vital to any real progress. Walesa felt that the workers could not entrust their interests to the Communist party. They had to look out for themselves. And the independent labor union, free from party interference, was the best way to accomplish that goal.

In 1975 tragedy struck: Lech Walesa's mother was killed suddenly while visiting in the United States. Of this he wrote: "All her life my mother wanted to go on a pilgrimage to the Black Madonna at the fourteenth-century Paulist monastery of Jasna Gora in Czestochowa. Instead of which she went to the United States, where she was killed in a traffic accident in 1975. She never did manage to make that particular dream come true."[10]

In 1976 Walesa was fired from his job at the Lenin shipyard for his political activism, and especially for making critical remarks about Edward Gierek, first secretary of the Communist party of Poland. He had accused Gierek of breaking his promises to the workers (see Chapter 3). An appropriate political joke was making the rounds in Poland that very year: Question: What is the difference between the United States and Poland? Answer: There is no difference at all. In America the people are completely free to criticize the President of the United States. And in Poland the people are also completely free to criticize . . . the President of the United States."

But the joke was not very funny for Walesa, who already had a large family to feed. Worse still, he found himself blacklisted, which meant that other factories were very reluctant to hire him. After a few months of searching in vain, he finally got a job as a mechanic at the transport division of Zremb, a construction supply factory.

Walesa continued his political activism at his new job as if nothing had happened. This showed both his intense determination and his courage. Knowing that it might mean losing his job again, he joined an underground Committee for Free Trade Unions of the Coastal Region. This group was active in convincing workers that their only hope of improving their lives was to ensure the creation of a free trade union independent of Communist party control. Other members included some people who later became famous as a result of the Solidarity strike of 1980—Anna Walentynowicz, Andrzej and Joanna Gwiazda, Kolodziej, Przybylski, and others. Walesa and his cohorts would meet in secret discussions, write and print up antigovernment leaflets, and pass them out to the workers or hang them up on walls. Eringer later wrote about this: "At the meetings of the Free Trade Unions movement, discussion centered on trade unions, human rights, workers' rights, contemporary history of Poland and the country's political situation. . . . Walesa would walk from one enterprise to the next, distributing leaflets and underground newspapers."[11]

During this time, the activities of the committee were constantly watched, and its members were frequently harassed by the security police. Walesa would sometimes stroll down the street with his newborn daughter Magdalena in her carriage. He would stop, pull out a few leaflets from under the baby's covers, and post them on a wall. Once, when he was caught doing this, the police had to take the baby home before they took Walesa to the police station for interrogation. He was usually released within the forty-eight-hour legal detention limit. One time when the police kept him longer than forty-eight hours, they apologized to him for detaining him illegally. They said they had been very busy that day and had just forgotten to let him go. He told them he understood and that they should not worry about it.

Walesa was elected to a workers' commission by his fellow workers at Zremb, where he continued to criticize the government. As a result, in December 1978, he was fired. Again Walesa had no job and no income.

The next few months were so hard that he had to sell his own makeshift van to get enough money to support his family. He also received contributions from underground donations to aid those who had been fired from their jobs for political reasons. Finally, in 1979, he was offered a job at a large electrical firm called Elektromontaz. Fearlessly he resumed his political activities. His determination was making him well known as an unusual individual who would stand up to the Communist authorities regardless of the personal cost. The Young Poland Movement, which had begun commemorating the anniversary of the 1970 slaying of striking workers from the Lenin shipyard, invited Walesa to speak at the site of the killings. He called for the building of a monument in their memory: "If not by government, then every person should bring one stone and we will pile these stones together and build this monument ourselves."[12] For his efforts, Walesa was fired from Elektromontaz just a few days before Christmas in 1979.

Walesa remained unemployed through the summer of 1980, when the workers of Gdansk went on strike to protest government price hikes. When Walesa heard that a strike had been declared, he rushed to join his former co-workers.

One of the first things the strikers demanded was the rehiring of Lech Walesa. The workers there greeted him enthusiastically, and Walesa soon became the leader of the Gdansk strike committee. The time had arrived to apply the lessons learned in past struggles.

CHAPTER 5

VICTORY IN GDANSK

The workers saw the huge discrepancies between what the Communist government told them and what it actually did. It was this gulf between the high ideals of socialist theory and the dire realities of everyday life which was the source of much popular antagonism toward the government.[1]

As with the strikes of 1970 and 1976, the main catalyst for the explosion of the workers in the summer of 1980 was government price hikes. On July 1 the official news agency announced that food prices in state-owned stores would go up dramatically. Meat, the main target of the price increase, nearly doubled in price overnight. This announcement of the price increase came suddenly and with no warning. It was presented in a matter-of-fact way on Polish television and radio, both of which were owned and operated by the state. There were no prior consultations with any worker organizations or their leaders. This infuriated the workers. The workers were barely able to make ends meet as it was; the government was now lowering their standard of living even further and doing so in a rather casual manner.

The whole postwar period had created the general climate for the strike for freedom in 1980: the dissatisfaction of the workers, their disillusionment with the promises of the government, the low standard of living, the corruption and waste of the system, the people's resentment of Soviet domination of Poland's political and economic life, and the experience of earlier social upheavals. The stage was set for massive social protest.

In retrospect, the decision of the authorities to raise prices again seems highly questionable, given the fact that so many of the major social upheavals of the recent past had been triggered by just such government action. Why would the government choose to open the wound again and risk another uprising by disgruntled workers? Was it so naive as to believe the workers would now passively accept price increases? The significant economic and financial pressure on government leaders for price reform must have outweighed, in their minds at least, the risk they knew they were taking by such measures. Perhaps they simply believed that they would have to go through a stormy social period, but in the end would get the price increases they desired. The workers would have no choice but to accept the decision. At worst, they might have to raise workers' salaries slightly in a number of factories in order to quiet social protest.

In actuality, the general economic stagnation of the country could not be ended without serious reform (see Chapter 3), and the government had little choice but to raise prices. As the first strikes were being declared, Mieczyslaw Rakowski, editor-in-chief of *Polityka*, a Communist weekly that represented the official party line, expressed this viewpoint: "We must tell the people the truth regarding the disastrous situation of the country. A program of radical reform is urgently needed."[2]

Contrary to a common misconception, the Gdansk shipyard was not the only factory in Poland to respond to the official announcement of price increases by calling for an immediate strike, nor was it even the first factory to go on strike. If Gdansk had been the only one, a Solidarity movement or an independent trade union probably would never have been born. In the weeks following the official announcement of the price increases, strikes and work stoppages broke out all over Poland. Within two months of the July 1 price increases, major strikes were declared in Lublin, Gdynia, Wroclaw, Jastrzebie, Katowice, Szczecin, Poznan, Lodz, Kielce, Cracow, Tarnow, Olsztyn, and many other smaller cities and towns. In spontaneous and sudden bursts of protest, factory workers throughout the country demonstrated their rejection of government policy.

Workers were really dissatisfied with much larger issues than the price of meat. These protests were essentially a vote of no confidence in the entire economic and political system. People were tired of listening to empty government promises. They no longer believed that a planned economy could provide them with the basic necessities of life in a reasonable manner. Meat became in large measure a symbol—a very important symbol to be sure, but a symbol nonetheless—of the government's failures. If the government could not put enough meat on the table for its citizens, then that government was not worthy of their respect. Perhaps the system was in need of serious economic reform, but this should not come at the workers' expense. And to prove their point, the workers were willing to go on strike.

Meat, especially ham, had long been the target of many political jokes through which Poles expressed their feelings. If they could not alter the situation, the very least they could do was to make fun of it. Here are some examples:

Before the war there used to be a sign outside the meat stores which read "Butcher," and inside one could find meat. Now in People's Poland, the sign outside the stores reads "Meat," but inside there is only the butcher.

A man goes into a store and asks, "Do you have any ham?" "No," comes the reply from behind the counter. "Do you have salami?" "No." He continues, asking in turn for bologna, sausage, veal, lamb, and many other cuts of meat.

Discouraged, he finally leaves empty-handed. The store worker looks at her co-worker and smiles. "That man must be crazy. We haven't had all those cuts of meat in here since the Communists took over after the war." "I know," says the other worker, "but what an incredible memory that man has."

In the summer of 1980 the workers were no longer laughing. The food crisis was threatening their families' well-being.

But economics was not the only issue on the minds of the workers. They also wanted basic political freedoms: freedom to gather publicly and express their opinions openly, freedom to get valid and accurate information from the mass media, freedom to criticize the policies of the government, and freedom to protest. Perhaps the economic issue was foremost, but whenever a confrontation with the government occurred, the issue of freedom was never forgotten. The workers always included it as one of their major demands. In fact, the economic and political issues were not really separate at all. Political freedom for the workers was the only way to ensure that their economic interests would be addressed. No one understood this better than the workers themselves. Lech Walesa and the other strike leaders were convinced of the need for free trade unions, independent of the government and the Communist party. This was a reform with profound economic implications for the workers as well as political implications for the authorities.

The irony of the July 1 price increases was that they were an attempt by the government to begin a measure of economic reform. For years the government had been subsidizing food consumption, artificially keeping the price of food below what it actually cost the government to bring it to market. While this tactic may have been politically useful, as it served to prevent worker unrest, it was only a temporary solution. It made no economic sense, and was soon to cause other economic problems, especially in the agricultural sector (see Chapter 3).

The government's call for this step in economic reform fell on deaf ears. By raising prices, the government was asking the people to endure more hardship and make more sacrifices, while it offered only the promise of vague future prosperity that perhaps only their grandchildren would see. Poles had heard it all so many times before. They remembered hearing it after the 1970 price increases, when the newly selected (not elected) party boss, Edward Gierek, implored the people to "help us help you." But in ten years Gierek had not helped them very much at all, as illustrated in the following joke:

Hundreds of people are standing in line in front of a meat store. Gierek is driving by in his fancy limousine and stops in front of the store. The people yell to him, "Mr. First Secretary of the Communist party, we have been standing in line for two days, waiting for a meat delivery." Gierek answers, "Comrades, I cannot bear to see you suffer like this. Let me help you." He drives away and a few minutes later, a huge truck pulls up in front of the store and they start unloading . . . chairs.

In 1980 the people wanted food, economic security, freedom, and justice, not another call for personal sacrifice. The system had to be made more responsive to the economic needs of the people. The government's failure meant that average citizens simply could not afford the higher cost of food. They demanded an immediate rollback of the price increases.

Over the course of the next few days, strikes became more and more numerous. Since most of the strikes were spontaneous reactions to the government's announcement, they were often hastily organized and uncoordinated. The specific demands of the workers varied from one factory to another according to that factory's working conditions, but all included either a rollback of the price increases or an increase in wages. Despite the occurrence of solidarity, or sympathy, strikes in which the workers in one factory would go on strike in support of the strike of their fellow workers from another factory, coordination on a national scale was lacking. Workers from one factory might be settling their strike while workers in another factory were just declaring their own. This lack of national coordination seemed to play into the hands of the authorities, who responded by negotiating with each factory on an individual basis. Usually, the management of a given factory, with government approval, would offer the workers a slight wage increase, hoping to get the strikers back to work without having to reduce prices to their former levels. In the long run, however, this policy served only to spread strike fever throughout the country. As word got around that striking workers were routinely being given wage increases, the logical conclusion for the employees of any given factory was to stage their own strike.

KOR, the Committee for Defense of Workers founded by Jacek Kuron and Adam Michnik after the strikes of 1976, played a significant role in this regard. The KOR organization served as the main link between workers and intellectuals in 1980. The day after the price increases went into effect, KOR announced its intention to serve as a strike-information clearinghouse. In this way, KOR helped to spread news of individual strikes to other areas of Poland and keep the workers informed as to their outcomes. It was the closest thing that the strikers had to some form of national coordination. KOR also helped to cement the alliance between dissident intellectuals and blue-collar workers, who now waged a common struggle against the ruling elite.

One of the first factories to go on strike was the tractor production plant at Ursus, not far from Warsaw, the same factory that had played a major role in the strikes of 1976. The workers laid down their tools almost immediately after the price decree and refused to go back to work until their demands were addressed. The government quickly agreed to grant them a wage increase of 10 to 15 percent, and they reluctantly returned to work. Sporadic strikes were called all over the country, and the pattern of quickly granting wage increases repeated itself. The government, eager to avoid a major showdown with the workers, in one case even granted a wage increase to workers in Radom before a strike was declared.

The city of Lublin was hit particularly hard by a massive wave of strikes in over thirty factories. The city was completely paralyzed. The authorities sent Deputy Premier Mieczyslaw Jagielski to negotiate with the strikers. Many of their demands were similar to the later demands of Lech Walesa's Solidarity strikers, with one major exception: the Lublin demands did not include the formation of free and independent trade unions. On July 20, the Lublin strikers went back to work after a compromise settlement was reached.

This happened the day after the Summer Olympics of 1980 had begun in Moscow. The United States was boycotting the Olympic Games to protest the Soviet invasion of Afghanistan. The invasion would soon become a key issue in Solidarity's political chess game with the government. Moscow was much less likely to interfere militarily in Polish affairs while it was already embroiled in another foreign war. World opinion had gone heavily against the Soviet Union for its invasion of Afghanistan; a new invasion of Poland would have led to near-universal condemnation and even severer economic sanctions. Perhaps even more significant, there were serious logistical problems in fighting two wars at the same time. The Poles were willing to gamble that Moscow would be reluctant to use its military power in Poland to crush worker unrest as long as the fighting in Afghanistan continued. They felt the Russians would prefer a political solution to the Polish question, and they were not mistaken. However, if things got totally out of hand, no one doubted for a moment that Soviet tanks would soon roll down the streets of Warsaw, Gdansk, Szczecin, and other major centers of political opposition.

The Afghanistan affair indicated how important a role international affairs, especially the superpower relationships, played in Poland's internal development.

On August 14, 1980, the workers at the Lenin shipyard in Gdansk also declared a strike. The next eighteen days were to change the history of Poland. In addition to the price hikes, an immediate cause of the Gdansk strike was the firing of a worker for her political activities. Anna Walentynowicz, a crane operator at the Lenin shipyard, was a longtime political dissident, a founder of the illegal Free Trade Unions movement, and friend of Lech Walesa. For some time the shipyard management had been looking for an excuse to fire her. One day she became ill on the job and went home to rest. She was fired for leaving her post without authorization. The workers demanded not only her reinstatement but also that of Lech Walesa, who had been fired four years earlier for his political activism.

As soon as Walesa learned of the strike declaration, he went to join his fellow workers, even though it had been years since he was fired. Because the shipyard was officially closed to nonemployees, Walesa secretly entered the grounds by jumping over a wall. The director and manager of the Lenin shipyard, Klemens Gniech, was talking to the workers, urging them back to work. Walesa walked right up to him in the middle of his speech and said, "Remember me? I worked here for ten years . . . it's four years since I lost my job."[3] Walesa quickly became the leader of the strike. At the time, he was thirty-six years old.

Walesa himself had nothing to do with the actual decision to declare a strike. In fact, he was not particularly happy about the timing of the strike. He thought that it came too soon and that the strikers were not fully prepared for it. But, sensing a political opportunity, he wholeheartedly supported it once it was declared. He said that "August was very inconvenient. I wanted to put the brakes on. After all, we weren't ready. There were no plans for afterwards. But, at the same time, we knew that if the social situation had come to a head we couldn't stand aside. We had to get involved. We wouldn't waste opportunities like they were wasted in 1956 and 1970. . . . But there was no 'orchestration' from me."[4]

The next day the government ordered a total communications blackout of Gdansk. All telephone lines were cut. Tadeusz Fiszbach, the local Party secretary, was sent to negotiate with the strikers.

On August 16, the Gdansk strike almost ended as the Lublin strikes had. During the initial negotiations the workers were offered a sizable wage increase, reinstatement of the fired workers, and even the right to build a monument to the slain workers of 1970. Except for the monument, this would have been purely an economic solution. Walesa nearly agreed to the terms, but at the last minute rejected them. He later claimed that this was only a political trick to oust radical hotheads from the strike committee, and that he never would have agreed to end the strike at that point.[5] The workers would continue the strike until their political demands were met. Above all, the government would have to allow the formation of an independent trade union.

There was another very important, more practical reason for continuing the strike. Neighboring factory workers and city employees, including bus and tram drivers in Gdansk, had also gone on strike. If the Gdansk shipyard workers had called off their strike and returned to work, after having concluded a separate agreement with the authorities, this would have undermined the position of the other strikers. These sympathy strikes, or strikes of solidarity, were becoming more common in Poland, aided by the organizational efforts of KOR, whose leaders were finally arrested on August 20. The workers at the Lenin shipyard wanted to continue their strike to demonstrate solidarity with their fellow striking workers in the Gdansk area. Only when their demands had been met would all the striking workers return to their jobs. Until that time, they would remain in the shipyard.

Soon a strike bulletin was being run off. It was called *Solidarity* (*Solidarność*) to indicate that all of the workers of Gdansk were united in a spirit of brotherhood. According to Walesa, it was actually Gniech, the shipyard director, who first referred to the strike in this way. The name caught on quickly, and soon the strikers referred to themselves and their entire social movement by this name. Copies of the strike bulletin were run off on a mimeograph machine in the shipyard printing office. Sometimes the quality was so poor that they were barely legible. Copies were also passed out to the crowds waiting outside the shipyard gates. People anxiously grabbed copies of the daily bulletin to learn the latest news on the strike.

The people outside the walls of the shipyard supplied

food to the striking workers. This happened spontaneously; no one organized it. Relatives of the strikers passed food daily through the fences and over the walls. Because it was impossible to give food individually to their own relatives, people simply handed the food to whomever was there to take it. They knew that someone else's food would find its way to their own son or husband, wife or mother.

Strike representatives from various places of employment in Gdansk and the surrounding area met and formed a special committee to coordinate their efforts. They called themselves the Inter-enterprise Strike Committee, or MKS. Lech Walesa was chosen as its acting chairman. The strike now encompassed much more than just the Gdansk shipyard. Strike representatives from all over the country began to petition for membership in the MKS. There were so many new members that the strike headquarters at the shipyard could not handle the flow of MKS representatives. By August 22 the MKS included representatives of over four hundred factories; its presidium, or ruling committee, had to reduce its number to one representative per factory simply to be able to hold a meeting.

In a complete departure from the pattern of previous social upheavals, Walesa openly welcomed the intellectual and dissident community into his strike committee. This marked the first time that the workers and intellectuals had acted together in opposition to government policies. About one week after the Gdansk strike was announced, a group of sixty-four intellectuals, many of whom were university professors, signed an open letter to the Communist party of Poland. In this letter they called upon the government to act with restraint, and they proposed peaceful negotiations with the strikers as a solution to the crisis. Two members of this group of sixty-four were sent directly to Gdansk to confer with and aid the Solidarity strike committee. They were Tadeusz Mazowiecki, editor of *Więź*, a Catholic magazine, and Bronislaw Geremek, a noted liberal historian. Geremek had also been involved in the creation of the flying universities set up after the 1976 strikes. Walesa wisely agreed to use their services in his negotiations with the government. Their expertise proved invaluable. Both men became very important figures in the Solidarity movement.

Walesa firmly refused to settle for economic concessions alone; regimes would come and go, and promises could be broken again. He knew that the workers really needed a permanent institution that would look after their interests. The essential point for Walesa and his fellow strike leaders was that there had to be free trade unions with the right to speak freely and organize their activities without interference from the government. Walesa had been fired repeatedly for criticizing the official Communist party–controlled trade unions and for his activism in the Free Trade Unions movement. This was not a new or spontaneous demand on his part, but a well-thought-out, long-standing goal. Walesa and his advisers were also uncompromising in their demand that the union be guaranteed the right to strike in the future. These decisions proved to be of unusual foresight, and they represented the most important element in the ultimate success of the Solidarity movement.

The government was willing to meet some of the workers' economic demands, but not their political ones. This strategy had worked in other cities. But the strike committee of Gdansk, under Walesa's leadership, had now seized a new opportunity. They had upped the stakes. The government was no longer in conflict with the workers merely over prices, wages, and working conditions. The conflict had now become one of power. Free trade unions and the right to strike meant moving out from under the control of the Communist party leadership. The question put to the government in Warsaw came down to this: Would the Communist party continue to control the political destiny of the country or would it share its power with an upstart political organization led by a dissident electrician who had massive popular support?

The workers in the shipyard became increasingly defiant and unruly. Chaos threatened to destroy the unity of the strikers, but Walesa knew what to do. The strike, he said, "kept collapsing every five minutes. I must have gone down to various sections at least five times, leading them in song, just to pick up the pieces again."[6] He sang patriotic and religious songs to raise their spirits and to strengthen their bond to each other in their common cause. The national anthem seemed an obvious choice: "Poland has not yet perished as long as we are alive. What a foreign power has taken away from us, we will regain with our swords." As they sang these words, they remembered the symbolism of the Dabrowski mazurka. They, too, were fighting for their freedom against a common foreign enemy, and as long as they were alive, there was hope of victory.

But there was one major difference between Walesa's strategy and that expressed in the national anthem: Walesa was firmly committed to a policy of *nonviolent* protest. The weapon the workers of Gdansk carried into battle was their willingness to go on strike. The strike, not the sword, was to be their means of restoring freedom and justice to their country. Every Polish citizen knew how to interpret the words of the national anthem this time. They understood that the foreign power which had imposed its rule on Poland and threatened its independence was the Communist party of the Soviet Union. However, with amazing restraint and political shrewdness, no Solidarity spokesperson said this publicly.

The immediate demand of the strikers, of course, was not Poland's complete independence from the Soviet Union but rather the establishment of free trade unions. But the two goals could not be kept separate indefinitely. To what degree would the trade unions really be free? Would they be free to reject the socialist economic programs of the Soviet Union? If the answer was yes, then clearly Poland would obtain a large measure of political freedom from Russian domination. Moreover, if Walesa is to be believed, his ultimate, though highly camouflaged, goal was in fact the total abolition of Soviet-style socialism in Poland (see Chapter 9). The real aspiration was once again Poland's freedom. Solidarity would start out by asking for free and independent trade unions while hoping ultimately to achieve national freedom.

The situation in Gdansk in the next few days became

extremely tense. It was feared that at any moment there would be a repeat of the 1970 violence. Anxious workers reacted to every noise, afraid that a police attack on the shipyard had begun. Walesa asked the strikers to remain on the shipyard grounds in a sit-in strike and do nothing to provoke the police. In contrast to the 1970 strike, this time there would be no street demonstrations and rioting, which could lead to violent confrontation with security forces. If the police stormed the shipyard, the workers were to remain seated on the floor and do nothing at all. Even if the police carried them out one by one, they were not to resist.

The government had no response to this tactical maneuver by the strikers. After a few days of wavering, it finally agreed to negotiate with the strike leaders. At this point there was a sigh of relief from Walesa and the strike committee. Now they knew there would not be a show of force. They would not be attacked by the police as long as the government's own representatives were on the shipyard grounds. Deputy Premier Mieczyslaw Jagielski, who had successfully negotiated an agreement during the Lublin strikes, was sent to repeat his performance in Gdansk. He and his delegation arrived at the shipyard on August 23 and were immediately presented with a list of twenty-one demands drawn up by the strike committee.

Here is a summary of the twenty-one demands made by the strikers:[7]

---

1. *Official recognition by the authorities of free trade unions independent of the Party and employers.*

2. *A guarantee of the right to strike and freedom from persecution for all strikers and their supporters.*

3. *A guarantee of freedom of speech and freedom of the press, including legal status for outlawed underground newspapers.*

4. *The reinstatement of the workers fired for defending workers' rights in the aftermath of the 1970 and*

1976 strikes, the reinstatement of all students expelled from universities because of their political activities, and the release of all political prisoners.

5. Publication and broadcast in newspapers, radio, and television, of news of the Interfactory Strike Committee and its demands.

6. The authorities to fully inform the public about Poland's socioeconomic status and to ensure open public participation in the reform program.

7. The workers should receive compensation for the time spent on strike at the rate of their normal holiday pay.

8. A salary increase of 2,000 zloty a month (about sixty-six dollars in terms of equivalent purchasing power at the time).

9. Automatic salary increase following increase in prices or currency devaluation.

10. Only surplus food should be exported; the food requirements of the Polish people should be met first.

11. Abolition of the system under which the best meat is sold in special shops at higher than official prices.

12. Introduction of a new management system whereby qualifications and merit are more important than Party membership; the abolition of special shops open only to police and Party officials.

13. Introduction of meat rationing until the market for meat is stable.

14. A lower retirement age: fifty-five for men, fifty for women, or a total of thirty years of service.

15. A standard-of-living increase in pensions and retirement benefits.

16. Improved work conditions for health service employees.

17. Improved standards for day-care centers and kindergartens.

18. Three years' full pay for maternity leave.

19. Shorter waiting periods for apartments.

20. Higher expense allowances for workers on travel assignment.

21. Saturdays off from work for everyone, or appropriate compensation for those who are required to work on Saturdays, including hospital employees and the like.

The first five demands were the truly important ones. They were the political demands which, taken as a whole, guaranteed freedom of political activity for their new organization. There would be no compromise on these points. Most of the rest were economic, and some were simply not within the power of the government to grant. The strike leaders certainly knew that not all of these demands could be fulfilled immediately, even if the government honestly wanted to do so. Most of the economic demands were therefore negotiable. But the first five were not.

Before long, however, negotiations were called off. The strikers demanded that before talks could continue, telephone lines in the area would have to be restored. This demand was met by the government a few days later, and talks resumed on August 26. By then the number of MKS delegates had grown to over one thousand. This meant that over a thousand factories in all parts of Poland had joined the strike organization in Gdansk. Meanwhile an increasing number of factory employees in Poland had joined in solidarity strikes with the workers of Gdansk. The strike spread all along the Baltic coast, including the shipyards of Szczecin, where separate negotiations with the government were taking place. Workers from the foundries in Cracow also announced their own strikes.

Support for the striking workers of Gdansk came from outside Poland's boundaries as well. Of particular interest to the people of Poland was what Pope John Paul II said about the matter. They listened intently to the Voice of America and BBC radio broadcasts. On August 20 they heard the pope speak for the first time about the crisis in his native land. His words gave the people of Poland renewed hope in their struggle: "We here in Rome are united with our fellow Poles whose problems are close to our heart and for which we ask the Lord's aid."[8] The words "We . . . are united with our fellow Poles" said it all. It was as if the pope had said "We are in solidarity with you." Everyone knew that the pope was with them in their struggle. The next day John Paul II dedicated Mass to a peaceful solution of the crisis in his homeland.

Jagielski and his delegation gradually realized what was at stake. They met frequently with government leaders in Warsaw to discuss a course of action. The government, to its credit, also wanted a peaceful solution to the crisis. The last time that Poles killed Poles in the suppression of a social upheaval, the government had fallen. They did not want a repeat of 1970; all sides hoped for a negotiated settlement.

The negotiations took place in a large room at the Lenin shipyard, at one long table in the center of the room. On one side of the table, the strike committee and its advisers sat in chairs several rows deep. Alongside Lech Walesa were such political activists as Andrzej Gwiazda, Bronislaw Geremek, and Bogdan Lis, who took an active role at the negotiating table. On the other side of the table sat the government delegation. The workers and the government were sitting face to face across the table. Klemens Gniech, the chief manager and director of the Lenin shipyard, and a member of the Communist party, was expected to sit with the government delegation. To the amazement of all sides, however, he sat on the side of the table with the striking workers. It was an indication of the immense popular support that the striking workers of Gdansk were about to receive.

Every word of the negotiations was broadcast live over the public address system to the masses of anxious workers waiting outside. Jagielski at first objected to this, but the strikers insisted. They had nothing to hide from their fellow workers, and in this way there could be no secret deals or coverups. In the spirit of true democracy, the workers could decide for themselves whether they approved of the course of the negotiations.

Mass was also celebrated daily on the shipyard grounds and many of the workers prayed for the success of the negotiations between the strike committee and the government delegation. Some of the devout workers identified their struggle with the Communist authorities as part of the struggle of their faith.

All of Poland anxiously watched the developments in Gdansk, fearful of a violent outcome. Support for the striking workers was widespread throughout Poland. In an unprecedented move, the authorities allowed the Western media to monitor the daily negotiations, and the whole world marveled at the courage and determination of the strikers.

Why did the government leaders allow the Western media to broadcast the events in Gdansk? Did this not aid their opponents? Perhaps, but they wanted to present a good face to the world. The government leaders wanted to show that they were not shooting at their citizens but talking with them. Poland was heavily dependent on Western technology and money. The last thing the government needed from the West was economic sanctions for repressing its people and violating human rights. Since it had decided in advance that a peaceful solution was preferable, why not let the world see that this in fact was the case?

Around August 26 the government's position took a turn for the worse. Sympathy strikes broke out in Silesia, an economically indispensable region of the country. It was the site of heavy industry, especially coal mines and steel works. It was also the home of Edward Gierek, head of the Communist party, and the area from which he drew most of his support. If he lost this power base, his position as party chief would be in jeopardy. Gierek was unable to prevent the strike fever from spreading throughout Silesia. Transportation workers from Wroclaw, miners from Jastrzebie, steel workers from Katowice, had all declared strikes as a show of solidarity with their Baltic colleagues. Under this overwhelming pressure, Gierek finally caved in and agreed to settle the Gdansk strike through negotiations; he consented in principle to the legal formation of an independent trade union. The Central Committee of the Communist party of Poland authorized Jagielski, as deputy premier of the nation, to make such an agreement with the workers. The agreement became known as the Gdansk Accords. The strike committee immediately chose Solidarity as the name of the new trade union. And to ensure that there would be no misunderstanding as to the legality of the new workers' union, Walesa also insisted that it be formally registered by the Polish courts so that Solidarity would have to be recognized as a legitimate social institution of Poland.

On August 31, 1980, eighteen days after the strike had begun, the two main representatives of the workers and the government, Walesa and Jagielski, signed the agreement at the Lenin shipyard. The strike leaders were not taking anything for granted. They asked Jagielski to initial each of the points individually, just to be sure there would be no doubt that he had agreed to every single provision in the agreement. To commemorate the occasion, Walesa used a huge souvenir pen, adorned with a picture of Pope John Paul II, to sign the Gdansk Accords. The new trade union would officially be called NSZZ Solidarność. The initials stood for Niezależne Samodzielne Związki Zawodowe, or the Independent Self-Governing Trade Union Solidarity.

After the signing ceremony, which was broadcast on public television, Walesa addressed the people of Poland: "My dear friends, we shall go back to work on September first. We fought not only for ourselves but for the future of our country. We obtained the right to strike, and most of all to form our own independent self-governing trade unions. Our new trade unions will begin tomorrow. I declare this strike over."[9]

At the end of his speech, Walesa sang the Polish national anthem, and even the government representatives joined in. There was jubilation throughout Poland. People cheered, sang, and hugged one another in the streets. It seemed to everyone that a major catastrophe had been avoided. The confrontation had ended not in bloodshed, as many had feared, but in a peaceful settlement. Nor had the Soviet Union interfered militarily. National unity had been preserved. Both sides knew that major problems lay ahead, but for now at least they could enjoy the success of the moment.

Not everyone was smiling, however. A few days later, on September 5, Edward Gierek was absent from a session of Parliament. It was reported that he was ill. The next evening, at a meeting of the Central Committee of the Communist party, he was replaced by Stanislaw Kania as head of the party. This was the government's way of saving face.

Once again striking workers of postwar Poland had toppled their government leadership. But this time there was a real political victory to go along with it. As Walesa himself admitted, the victory of the workers was not total, but it was a huge step in the right direction.

CHAPTER 6

FIREMAN LECH

There was no manual of instructions telling me what I had to do and how.[1]

LECH WALESA

CONCESSIONS

The striking workers of Gdansk had won many concessions from the government on August 31, 1980. The most important was government recognition of their right to form independent trade unions with the right to strike. The government had also made other promises. These included improved health and working conditions, Saturdays free from work, a relaxation of censorship rules, the release of political activists from jail, and open access to the mass media. The Gdansk Accords of 1980 also granted the right to have Sunday Mass broadcast every week on official state radio. This was no small concession by a government that was supposed to be atheistic. It was widely known that some Communist party members themselves went to Mass on Sunday. This, of course, was frowned upon, but there was little the government could do about it. The Party was clearly losing the battle for the social conscience of the people. When asked what Solidarity's major achievement had been, Marian Jurczyk, chairman of Solidarity in Szczecin, said it was this concession by the government that allowed Sunday Mass to be broadcast on the radio.[2]

Another of the most noteworthy concessions the strikers received from the government in 1980 was permission to build a monument to the slain workers of 1970. Walesa personally pushed the government very hard on this particular point. He felt the loss of his co-workers in 1970 very deeply, believing that somehow he might have been partially responsible for the failures of the 1970 strike. If only he had known more, if only he had done things differently. Neal Ascherson, noted writer on Polish matters, goes so far as to say: "This obsession with the martyred dead, so much a part of the national psychology, was the source of his driving anger and his obstinacy."[3]

The building of the monument, therefore, was a personal triumph for Walesa, a vindication of the slain workers and their families, a statement that they had not suffered and died in vain. The monument meant that they would always be remembered and appreciated by their countrymen for having given their lives in the struggle for a better Poland. It was almost a religious expression of gratitude, and its symbolism was not hard to find. The monument itself is three large crosses with anchors resting on them, all joined with one another. The anchors symbolize much more than the workers' occupation as shipbuilders. Each anchor is in the shape of the letter *P* on top and *W* on the bottom. PW stands for *Polska Walcząca,* "Poland Is Still Fighting," the motto of the Polish Home Army, which led the partisan resistance to Hitler's occupation. The anchors rest on the crosses as if crucified. This symbolizes the martyrdom of the slain workers. These men were crucified in the struggle to save Poland.

On December 16 of every year, on the anniversary of their death, Poles ritually honor the slain workers at this monument. And Lech Walesa has always been there with them:

There's 16 December. That's my day. Because I was the one who was instrumental in putting that monument up. I sat in [jail] longer than anyone else to get it. And every man, woman and child in Poland will know—write this down—that every year, on 16 December, I will be at that monument. . . . There is no power on earth that will stop me doing that. And there, under that monument, we'll rehearse all we have to say to each other. And it will be there, if the need arises, that we'll set up free unions once again.[4]

The workers, too, had made certain concessions to the government in the Gdansk agreement. For one thing, Solidarity did not get all of its economic demands. In fact, it settled for a much lower pay raise than the one that had been offered on August 16, the day their strike almost ended prematurely. Politically, the union also had to recognize the "leading role of the Communist party" in Poland, and it had to state that it would not oppose the existing system of international alliances, known as the Warsaw Pact. Since everyone knew that the Warsaw Pact was dominated by the Soviet Union, this last point was meant to reassure Moscow that Solidarity would not threaten its power.

In order to reassure Moscow further, Solidarity also reaffirmed a belief in socialism; at the very least, Solidarity would not object to the fundamental socialist principle of public ownership of the means of production. In the following weeks, Walesa was to say publicly many times that Solidarity was not against socialism. Rather, it and he were for a better socialism, a more just and democratic socialism (see Chapter 9). He also repeatedly stated that Solidarity was neither a political organization nor a political party; it was a trade union that dealt primarily with economic, not political, issues. This language, however, was used to reassure the Communist party of both Poland and the Soviet Union that Solidarity would not threaten the existing socialist form of government. In reality there was no denying that Solidarity was involving itself in politics.

The government also objected to the use of the name, the Free Trade Union Solidarity. That implied that the old Communist-controlled trade unions were not free, a fact the government refused to admit. After much haggling over this issue, it was decided to use instead the name Independent Self-Governing Trade Union Solidarity (NSZZ Solidarność). Walesa was careful to use the appropriate words in his speeches.

THE SOURCES OF SOLIDARITY'S IDEALS

Lech Walesa and other workers in Poland, as well as Polish intellectuals and dissidents, got the ideas and philosophy behind their movement from a number of sources. One source was rooted in Polish history: the liberal tradition, which stresses the idea of freedom.

By listening to Radio Free Europe, the British Broadcasting Corporation (BBC), and the Voice of America, Poles also learned about Western democracies. Strictly speaking, they were forbidden to listen to these programs, which gave Western versions of events, but the authorities were powerless to prevent it, and most just looked the other way.

Travel and tourism served as another source of Western ideas. Tourists were a much needed source of Western currency, and thousands of tourists, many of Polish descent (the Polonia), flocked to Poland every year, bringing with them not only money but also tales of life in Western Europe and America. Even in a semi-totalitarian society like Poland, many citizens were allowed to travel abroad, unlike the residents of other countries in the Soviet bloc, which were much more closed and restricted. Many Western books were brought into Poland by tourists and travelers, sometimes illegally.

Western labor union movements became a source of ideas about workers' rights and political strategies for Solidarity. In a speech in Geneva in June 1981, Walesa spoke to the International Labour Conference: "When in August 1980 we decided to create independent, self-managed trade unions, we used in full the provisions of the ILO Conventions Nos. 87 and 98 on freedom of association and trade union rights to strengthen Solidarity."[5]

Another major source of Western ideas in Poland was the philosophical and religious teachings of the Catholic church. The philosophy behind the Solidarity movement had its roots in church tradition. From the start, Walesa linked the struggle of the workers to the church. When addressing the workers, he often spoke of the values he had learned during his Catholic upbringing—the dignity of work, human rights, and moral justice—the same topics that the pope often mentioned in his sermons to Poles. Another source of ideas was Jesuit social philosophy, especially the ideas of the German social economist Heinrich Pesch. Pesch saw society as a union of many free and individual members in a common moral bond, a community of free citizens striving for the welfare of all. This included the development of values that encouraged responsibility and private enterprise, rejecting a compulsory planned economy and recognizing the importance of economic freedom. These were the kinds of values the Catholic church instilled in its members, and through its teachings, they became part of the Polish value system and the Solidarity movement.

The importance of the church to the striking workers of the Gdansk shipyard cannot be overemphasized. For example, the strikers immediately demanded and got the right to have priests brought into the shipyards to say daily Mass for the workers. The government agreed to this partly because it hoped the church would have a calming effect upon the workers. In other words, the government knew the church would preach a message of nonviolence. Another indication of the importance of the Catholic church to the Solidarity movement can be seen in the person of Lech Walesa himself. He was a deeply religious man who often looked to the church for guidance. During this entire period, Walesa never failed to consult with representatives from the church. His parish priest from Gdansk, Father Henryk Jankowski, was much more than just his priest. He was Walesa's close friend and adviser, a man to whom he looked for spiritual guidance as well as practical advice. Father Jankowski also served as Walesa's link to the church hierarchy.

In linking the struggle of the workers to the church, Walesa remained true to Polish tradition and culture. Throughout the strike, and for many months thereafter, Walesa appeared wearing two items pinned to the lapels of his suit jacket: a Solidarity button on the right side and a small badge with a picture of the Black Madonna on the left. The religious and political symbolism of the Black Madonna was not lost on Lech Walesa and the other striking workers of the Gdansk shipyard. They believed that she would once again aid Poles in their struggle for freedom. In fact, in almost all of Walesa's public appearances, the Black Madonna was pinned on the front of his suit jacket, a sign for all Poles to see and understand.

A NEW STRUGGLE BEGINS

The period between the victorious outcome of the Gdansk strikes on August 31, 1980, and the declaration of martial law on December 13, 1981, marked the first stage of Solidarity's existence. During those sixteen months, one fact became increasingly apparent. The victory in August was really only the beginning of a new struggle for the Polish workers; it was not the end of a long process. Later developments would prove that the government was not acting completely in good faith. In order to end the immediate crisis, the government promised more than it was actually willing to give. Communist leaders probably assumed that they could, after things calmed down, reduce or alter the number of points they had conceded. The authorities tried to thwart Solidarity at every turn, hoping to remove some of the power they had reluctantly given the trade union just to get the strikers back to work.

The legal registration of the Solidarity trade union, for example, turned into a major crisis. When Lech Walesa and his delegation went to Warsaw to start the official registration process, they were met with an unpleasant surprise. The district court, without notifying or consulting with Solidarity, had added some new clauses. Solidarity now had to include in its bylaws the official recognition of the "leading role of the Communist party in Poland" and the acceptance of "existing international alliances." The union also had to accept certain limitations on its right to strike. It was one thing to accept these principles in the Gdansk agreements ending the strike, but it was quite another to include them formally in the legal statutes of the new trade union.

Solidarity members were outraged that their Gdansk agreement with the government had been changed in this arbitrary way by the judge. They considered it illegal, and they felt that these amendments eliminated any hope of having truly independent trade unions. How could a trade union be truly independent and self-governing if it had to submit by law to the higher authority of the Communist party? This would make a mockery of the words "independent and self-governing." The workers chanted over and over, "No decision about us without us," reminding many of the American Revolutionary slogan, "No taxation without representation." Many members of Solidarity, including Anna Walentynowicz and the more radical delegates, were prepared to break off all negotiations and immediately declare another strike.

Walesa, however, argued for moderation. He wanted to use normal legal channels and appeal the decision of the district court in the Polish Supreme Court. But even he threatened to call for a renewed strike if the matter could not be resolved. Solidarity adopted Walesa's moderate approach, and that proved to be a wise tactical maneuver. The Supreme Court reversed the lower court decision, and Solidarity was officially registered on November 10, 1980. The country was saved from another series of strikes that might have erupted in violence, and Walesa's position was reinforced.

The fact that the Supreme Court of a Communist country sided with the opposition group in the settlement of a legal matter is a strong statement of the respect for law in Poland.

A completely totalitarian government would simply have directed the Supreme Court to rule in its favor. This respect for legal principles is a trait seen throughout the Solidarity struggle. The government would use tricks and political maneuvers, but it would not openly defy the laws of the land in front of the entire Polish nation.

By September 17, membership in Solidarity had risen to about 3 million people, with many new workers joining every day. After a one-hour warning strike on October 3 in which the entire nation participated, its membership quickly grew to 6 million. At its peak, about 10 million Poles belonged to Solidarity. This represented approximately one-half the work force in a country of about 36 million people—a staggering number. Even members of the Communist party deserted their former posts and joined Solidarity. It was estimated that one-third of all members of the PZPR, the Polish Communist party, joined the new trade union. The whole society, or so it seemed, was rushing to join the union.

The Gdansk Accords had given the workers of Poland the right to strike, and they began to use it with a vengeance. Years of pent-up frustrations now seemed to find a universal outlet; whenever the workers were dissatisfied, they could declare a strike. In the first few months after the Gdansk strike, Walesa was often forced to play the role of a mediator. He traveled from one end of the country to the other to end a series of rash strikes that threatened to disrupt the country. He felt that Poland needed time to adjust to the new situation. The country did not need any more social unrest that would put Solidarity's gains in jeopardy. His very presence was often enough to persuade the workers to go back to work. But sometimes he had to spend long hours in heated debates with local strike committees.

Some of the strikes were totally justified. Local Communist party officials were often unwilling to grant their workers the rights that had been won in Gdansk, because that meant giving up some of their power. And sometimes people were even unaware that the Gdansk agreements applied to all of Poland. But more frequently strikes were used as the first means of settling any complaint the workers had with their employers. Walesa tried to explain to them that they were abusing the right to strike. It should not be a first resort but a last resort, after all other methods had failed. But the newfound freedom to strike was hard to resist. The workers had never had it before. So Walesa continued his journeys around the country, trying to keep things under control.

Walesa was so successful in persuading the workers to end their strikes and to allow the Gdansk Accords to operate in a calm and peaceful environment that he was given the nickname "fireman of Poland." Hardly a day passed when he wasn't "putting out a fire" somewhere in the country.

On the economic front, however, food shortages were becoming more and more severe. It was widely rumored that the government was deliberately allowing the economic crisis to take place in the hope of showing that Solidarity's influence was only hurting the economy. Stores were almost completely empty. One food store had nothing on its shelves but jars of pickles. Another, nothing but canned beets. Another, nothing at all. The employees milled around in the stores reading or talking. They had nothing to do but wait for a delivery. When deliveries did arrive, huge lines formed even before the goods could be unloaded. It was commonplace to wait two or three hours just to buy a half kilo (about one pound) of butter. Meat was becoming so scarce that on April 1, 1981, a program of meat rationing went into effect. Poles jokingly remarked that this was only a cruel April Fools' prank. Meanwhile Poland's foreign debt grew larger and larger as the nation borrowed more money from the West just to keep the economy afloat. By April 1981 the national debt had reached $25 billion.

A very frightening and dangerous incident occurred in Bydgoszcz on March 19, 1981, when the security police broke up a meeting of Solidarity representatives. In the violence, many Solidarity activists were hurt. Jan Rulewski, a Solidarity spokesman for the Bydgoszcz region, was hospitalized along with two others. Solidarity demanded an investigation into the incident. Who had given the orders for such action? Unless those responsible for the beatings were punished, Solidarity threatened another general strike. The entire incident served only to increase tensions dramatically between the government and Solidarity. A compromise solution was finally reached when Walesa personally conferred with Deputy Prime Minister Mieczyslaw Rakowski. A four-hour warning strike was called. But there would be no general strike, which would have paralyzed the country and made a military response by the government more likely.

SOLIDARITY'S DILEMMA

To what degree could the issue of free trade unions be kept separate from the demand for Poland's national freedom? This question created a serious dilemma for Solidarity over the issue of moderation versus radical change. The membership was split on two issues: the speed of change and the degree of change. The heart of the dilemma was really very simple. Real freedom for the workers could not be separated from Poland's political freedom from the Soviet Union. Yet political freedom from the Soviet Union did not seem to be a possibility.

In 1980 few people dreamed that their social protest would eventually lead to the complete overthrow of the Communist party in Poland.[6] On any realistic grounds, this outcome seemed utterly impossible. It was believed that the Soviet Union and the entire Communist leadership of East Central Europe would never allow it. This assumption seemed entirely reasonable, and it was not seriously questioned by political analysts from either the West or the East. While Poles might hope to reform the existing system, no one, least of all the Poles themselves, expected it to be overthrown. For this reason Solidarity would describe itself as "a self-limiting movement."[7] It wanted a significant measure of change, but knew it had to operate within the realm of existing political possibilities. So the goal of Lech Walesa and other Solidarity leaders in 1980 and 1981 had to be limited to serious economic reform, coupled with a demand for increased democratization of society.

THE SOCIAL ALLIANCES OF SOLIDARITY

One of the interesting facts about the rise of Solidarity is that its members came from all sectors of Polish society. Factory workers, students, intellectuals, Catholic clergy, farmers, scientists, and even bureaucrats became staunch supporters of Solidarity and fierce opponents of the government. Overwhelming forces of moral opposition were amassed against the Communist party. With historical hindsight it now seems clear why the government eventually decided to give in to the demands of the Gdansk strikers in 1980. Never before had all these forces of Polish society acted together, united in their opposition. The government, however, had the military and police force behind it, combined with the ultimate threat of Soviet intervention to protect the Communist party of Poland. In other words, the government had control of the weapons of physical force, but Lech Walesa and Solidarity had the hearts and minds of the people. In the long run, the people were victorious; moral force proved superior to physical force.

Given this tremendous popular support, we can now see that the belief in the ability of the Solidarity movement to stand up to the government in 1980 was perhaps not so naive after all. But this unity did not materialize overnight. Many years of failure had paved the way for success in 1980.

One of the main reasons for the success of Solidarity in August 1980 was the fact that Lech Walesa had skillfully manipulated supporters from various sectors of the society. Of particular importance was the worker-intellectual alliance. Walesa said of this alliance: "Take, for example, the question of involving the academics in the strike. Today, people are saying that Solidarity is a veritable model of the alliance between the workers and the intelligentsia. A model which can teach the rest of the world."[8]

Walesa went on to explain that when he put writers and novelists on the strike committee presidium in 1980, he faced much opposition from workers strongly opposed to that strategy. He said that "nobody cares to remember how I was reviled for getting the academics involved in the strike. I had to do that because I wanted to have as many social groups as possible represented. And what did some of the others say? No, let me refresh your memories. They said that we should send all those intellectuals to the devil, that we would be able to manage on our own, and that we would show them just how much we can do without anyone's help. That's the way it was. . . ."

To this worker-intellectual alliance Walesa added the moral power of the Catholic church, which he used at every opportunity to gain support for his social movement. Even the farmers joined in the protest movement and demanded the right to form their own independent trade union.

THE CREATION OF RURAL SOLIDARITY

The agricultural situation in Poland was very important in explaining the failure of the Communist economic system and the widespread unrest that led to the creation and success of Solidarity. Poland was still overwhelmingly dominated by small private farms owned and operated by individual peasant households. The state's agricultural policies had often directly hindered the private farmers. Since the state's goal was to eventually introduce socialist agriculture, it did not care about the interests of the peasant landowners. The state's economic policies had also resulted in low prices for agricultural goods. Farmers found themselves in an absurd economic position. It sometimes cost more to produce a certain crop than they could get for selling it to the state collection centers. There was little incentive to produce. Stories were common about farmers who bought bread at the state-owned stores to feed to their pigs because that was sometimes cheaper than growing grain. This irrational economic situation angered the peasants, but they had never really channeled their anger into an effective political response. The success of the Gdansk strike changed all that.

The alliance of peasants and workers did not play a significant role in the Gdansk strikes of 1980 or in the creation of Solidarity. But that alliance did have an enormous effect on the ultimate success of the movement. The peasants added one more social voice to those that were raised against the economic policies of the government. Soon after the victory of the workers in Gdansk, the peasants began talking about forming their own free trade unions. Modeling themselves after Solidarity, they called for the creation of Rural Solidarity. Just as Solidarity would defend the interests of the workers, Rural Solidarity would look out for the interests of the farmers. In the middle of December over one thousand angry farmers met in Warsaw to seek formal recognition by the government.

The government was very reluctant to give in on this point. It was one thing to grant independent trade union status to workers in factories owned by the state. It was quite another matter to do the same for individual peasant farmers who owned their own land. To understand this, it is necessary to discuss the issue in terms of the socialist transformation of Poland. The Communist party of Poland was operating, for the most part, according to the same Marxist-Leninist guidelines as the Soviet Union. Marx regarded peasants as backward rural idiots who would never willingly accept a socialist transformation. He believed that the socialist revolution would come from the urban factory workers, not from the peasants.

Communists assumed that the socialist transformation of society would include the collectivization of agriculture, the combining of small peasant farms into large cooperative farms. The Polish Communist party saw this as an essential step in establishing a socialist economy. If, however, each peasant household held its own land as private property and formed a union to defeat collectivization, there could be no socialist system. If the Polish Communist party gave in to the farmers, it would be rebuked by the Soviets, who had collectivized agriculture years before and who insisted that their experience be copied in Poland and other East Central

European countries. Therefore, the Polish government was determined to resist any attempt by Polish farmers to create a rural version of Solidarity.

The result was a prolonged confrontation between the government and private farmers. In January 1981 farmers occupied the state agricultural offices in Rzeszów, a city in southeast Poland. They demanded the recognition of Rural Solidarity. In March of the same year Rural Solidarity, having organized itself even without formal government permission, held its first congress in Poznan. The government eventually decided it could not hold out any longer. Registration of the farmers' union took place in Warsaw in May 1981. Rural Solidarity was now a legal institution.

THE CHURCH, THE PARTY, AND SOLIDARITY

Three institutions, above all others, have shaped today's Poland: the Communist party, the Solidarity trade union, and the Roman Catholic church. The Communist party began to play a significant role in the political and economic life of the country after World War II. Solidarity did not even come into existence until 1980. The church has played a major role in all aspects of Polish society since the tenth century. The interaction of these three different institutions ultimately shaped the existing state of affairs in Poland. In late 1980 and throughout 1981 the leaders of this triumvirate—church, Party, and trade union—became the real power brokers of the country.

Of the three major social institutions of Polish society, two of them—the church and Solidarity—were united in their opposition against the third, the Communist party. The party was thus outnumbered two to one. But before it caved in completely, it made several attempts at a comeback. One of them came on December 13, 1981, when the Party chief, General Wojciech Jaruzelski, as head of the government, declared a state of martial law in Poland. The social tension and political stress created by this forced "power sharing" might have been the reason for the government's decision to declare martial law. Solidarity was banned, and Lech Walesa and the other Solidarity leaders were placed under arrest. As long as the Communist party had the threat of Soviet military intervention to back it up, the odds were really two to two. The result was a political stalemate that continued until 1989.

CHAPTER 7

MARTIAL LAW

***I should like to express our solidarity with working people throughout the world; with the struggle waged by trade unions in defence of the social interests of the working people, in defence of dignity of work, for the protection of human rights wherever they are being infringed.*[1]**

LECH WALESA

MARTIAL LAW

On December 13, 1981, General Wojciech Jaruzelski appeared on state-owned television and radio to announce a state of emergency throughout the country. A few weeks before, he had replaced Stanislaw Kania as head of the Communist party. Now, in his triple role as leader of the Communist party, head of the government, and commander in chief of the army, he officially declared a state of martial law. This meant that Polish law would be suspended indefinitely, that new restrictions on citizens and foreign residents would go into effect immediately, and that the army would enforce them.

The new restrictions severely limited freedom of movement. Travel outside the city or village in which one lived was forbidden. Special permission had to be obtained for any exceptions. Curfews were imposed to prevent people from gathering on the streets or hiding their activities under the cover of darkness. No persons were to be outside their homes after 10:00 P.M. Anyone found violating the new rules could be arrested on the spot. The forty-eight-hour detention limit that had protected political dissidents in the past was suspended. The government now could hold people in prison for as long as it wanted without bringing formal charges. It did not even have to give a reason.

To prevent student unrest, universities and colleges were temporarily closed, and when they reopened they were supervised by army officers. The same was true of many factories. Tanks and military vehicles rolled through the streets, and the police set up checkpoints at key intersections. Roadblocks were also set up on all major thoroughfares leading in and out of most cities and towns. Special riot police, called ZOMO, were stationed in areas where social disturbances might occur. They were dressed in full riot gear, including helmets, shields, and nightsticks.

Transportation and mass media were placed under strict military control. Workers in these areas were treated like soldiers in the army during a war. Any attempt at a strike could be considered desertion, and strict military punishment could follow. In theory, workers came under the same strict rules as soldiers in time of war. That's why it was called martial law. For example, a gas station attendant who left his station without permission could be arrested, court-martialed, and even shot for deserting his post. As it turned out, extreme measures were never taken, but at the time no one was sure just what would happen.

Censorship was legalized. Telephone lines were strictly monitored. All newspapers were shut down except for the military newspaper, *Żołnierz Wolności*. (Ironically, its title meant "Soldier of Freedom.") Within days other newspapers were allowed to resume publication, but only under army supervision and strict government censorship.

All international and domestic flights were canceled, except for military planes. Poland's borders were closed. No one was allowed to enter or leave without special permission. Tourists already in Poland had to leave as soon as their visas expired. No new visas to enter Poland were issued, but foreigners on work permits, foreign students, and the diplomatic staffs of foreign embassies were allowed to remain in the country. (The international status of the diplomats made them immune from the travel restrictions and curfews.)

It seemed that the victory of Solidarity had been abruptly reversed. Thousands of Solidarity leaders across the country were arrested. Lech Walesa was flown to Warsaw in a military helicopter for "questioning." As he was leaving the house, he told his wife, Danuta, that he would be back soon. Instead, he was interned by the government in a special form of arrest. The government wanted to work out some sort of deal with him, but he flatly refused to negotiate. He demanded that Cardinal Wyszynski be present before he would engage in talks with the authorities. Eventually he was allowed visitors, including special representatives from the Catholic church, with whom he frequently conferred. In all, he spent about thirteen months in confinement.

The reaction in Poland to the imposition of martial law was shock, surprise, and anger. The announcement came about two weeks before Christmas, when most Poles were busily preparing for the holidays. They were psychologically unprepared for such a turn of events, a fact the Communist regime was counting on to make the people easier to control. Street demonstrators were greeted by ZOMO, the special riot police, with water cannons. Some strikes were called. But because its leaders were already under arrest, Solidarity's resistance was ineffective. The army and ZOMO were staring them in the face, so there was really very little they could do. The government had won this round.

Miners in Silesia did strike. They remained down in their mines and demanded an immediate end to martial law. The miners spent Christmas underground, separated from their families. A few were killed in confrontations with the police.

Gradually, however, the miners came to the surface, and the strikes at the mines ended.

Martial law was very well organized and well planned. Many Poles sarcastically suggested that if the Polish economy were only half as well planned and executed as martial law, the country would have been living in material abundance. It seemed incredible that arrangements for such a huge operation could have been kept a secret. Even American intelligence networks may not have picked up the advance signals until it was too late to do anything about it.

Public sentiment at the time was very anti-Jaruzelski. He was called a traitor, a man who had made war on his own people. There was a feeling that eventually he would be made to pay for this crime. A widely heard joke had Jaruzelski staring at himself in a large mirror hanging on the wall. He looked at the image of himself and said, "General Jaruzelski, what have we done? What will become of us?" The image in the mirror smiled back and replied, "That's easy. They'll take me down and they'll hang you up."

Years later, however, people realized that under Jaruzelski's leadership the enforcers of martial law had shown a great deal of restraint. Very few people were killed or injured. Many people also came to believe that Jaruzelski's actions probably prevented a Soviet invasion of Poland. Many Poles came to the conclusion that "if the Poles did not straighten things out for themselves, the Russians would do it for them." Leonid Brezhnev was head of the Soviet Union at the time, and he was much more willing to use force than his successor, Mikhail Gorbachev, would be. Jaruzelski may quite possibly have saved Poland from much bloodshed by imposing martial law when he did. Despite these facts, however, much public resentment toward Jaruzelski remained.

Zbigniew Brzezinski, a Polish-American statesman and adviser to President Jimmy Carter, agreed with this assessment of possible Soviet intervention. In fact, Brzezinski had received certain intelligence information about a Warsaw Pact meeting in Moscow that had been called specifically to discuss the problem of social unrest in Poland. Apparently the

Soviets were seriously debating the issue of direct military intervention in Poland. Brzezinski tried to warn such Western allies as Great Britain, France, and West Germany, as well as the Solidarity leadership, that a Soviet invasion was a distinct possibility. Solidarity believed it highly unlikely that the Russians would send in their armies. Brzezinski's message was that perhaps this belief was a delusion.

Walesa's reputation as the leader of the opposition forces in Poland was greatly enhanced by the coverage he received in the Western media. Many Poles felt that someone else might have been better qualified than Walesa in this role, but his reputation in the West served a valuable purpose. The Western press had made Lech Walesa the symbol of resistance against communism in Poland; no one else could easily replace him. Moreover, no other living Pole except Pope John Paul II had such high visibility in the Western press, and no other Pole was instantly recognized around the world. Everyone knew of Lech Walesa. He could get an audience with important leaders everywhere. This recognition in the West increased his stature and leadership position back in Poland.

The culmination of this process came in 1983, when he was awarded the Nobel Peace Prize, an award that was extremely honored and well respected in Poland. As a result, Walesa's stature as a true political hero grew in his home country. Although he could have been greeted in Norway during the awards ceremony as a great political hero, with international news coverage, Walesa refused to leave Poland to accept his Nobel Prize. He feared that the authorities might not let him return to Poland if he left the country. His wife, Danuta, went to Norway in his place and accepted the award for her husband.

The imposition of martial law temporarily saved the power of the Communist party in Poland. But the new regime under General Wojciech Jaruzelski was faced with problems it could not hope to solve, since it did not have the support of the people. The party now wanted to reform the economic system while leaving the political system intact. It tried to introduce certain elements of a free market economy while preserving the monopoly of power of the Communist party. The result, however, was that neither the economy nor the political structure worked very efficiently, and the entire Polish Communist state entered into a further decline.[2]

Martial law was officially lifted in July 1983, although some of its specific restrictions remained in force for some time. The government wished to return to a state of normalcy, whatever that was. Gradually, the society began to focus more on everyday life and less on political issues. Solidarity remained banned by law. Its charter had been revoked. The government now cynically referred to Walesa as "the former head of a former trade union."

STALEMATE

"Stalemate" is a good word for the political situation between the government and Solidarity in Poland from 1983 to 1989. Solidarity had received strong support from many parts of Polish society. Factory laborers, Catholics, intellectuals, students, and peasants were all anti-regime and anti-Communist. The government simply had no political legitimacy other than the right to use force, backed up by the threat of Soviet intervention if the situation got out of hand. Many Soviet troops were already stationed in Poland. Their presence had been felt since the end of the Second World War. Although they did not make themselves conspicuous, the fact that they were in Poland made the people aware that if it became necessary, Soviet troops could be used.

Solidarity was forced to go underground. A Temporary Coordinating Committee (known as TKK) was formed. In this way, Solidarity sympathizers were able to continue their political activism. The hard-core Solidarity members remained totally committed to their cause. Many Poles, however, grew apathetic. People increasingly preferred to concentrate on their own lives and the hardships of daily existence. People frequently remarked, "We are simply too tired, too physically and emotionally exhausted, to openly engage in any more resistance." They still gave their passive support to the Solidarity underground, but many of them were very pessimistic that anything would come out of the movement. This "fatigue of Solidarity supporters" eventually took its toll.

This period of apathy and stagnation after martial law lasted for a number of years. According to the official sources, alcoholism, drug abuse, and crime — including violent crime — were on the increase, and the visitor to Poland was struck by the number of drunks and drug addicts in the streets, many of them young people.[3] The joy and exhilaration of 1980 and 1981 were gone. After managing their daily lives, people were too tired to think much about politics.

A general amnesty for Solidarity activists was proclaimed by the government in July 1983 and again a year later. This amnesty included people under political arrest as well as activists still in hiding, providing they turned themselves in to the authorities. The most famous of the Solidarity activists in hiding in the underground movement was Zbigniew Bujak from Warsaw. He managed to avoid capture throughout this entire period.

In October 1984 a pro-Solidarity priest, Father Jerzy Popieluszko, was murdered by four officers of the security police. Over a quarter of a million people attended the funeral, at which Archbishop Józef Glemp of Cracow officiated. This proved to be something of a turning point. The outrage that the ordinary Polish citizen felt over this crime was immense. It became the universal topic of conversation in Poland, and it clearly put the government on the defensive. David S. Mason reported that "Buttons, pictures and postcards of Popieluszko are in churches everywhere, and his church and burial site, Saint Stanislaw in Warsaw, has become a virtual shrine, with a constant stream of visitors and pilgrims."[4] One political analyst even wrote an article entitled: "Now Solidarity Has a Martyr."[5] The Jaruzelski government gave in to public sentiment, and in 1985, the four officers were tried for murder. They were found guilty and received long prison sentences, but the damage had already been done. Relations between the state and society continued to sour.

By 1985, although popular defiance and open resistance

to the government were not as strong as they had been in 1980 to 1981, the regime was still not able to engage the people actively in the process of economic reform.[6] People, especially the younger generation, had become increasingly disillusioned with politics, and many of them were even indifferent toward Solidarity and Walesa. Walesa used the period of stalemate to organize his underground forces, although constant police monitoring made this very difficult. It was at this time also that he wrote his autobiography, *Droga nadzieji,* or *A Way of Hope.*[7]

A mild turning point came in June of 1987, when Pope John Paul II made a second pilgrimage to Poland. This time he went to Gdansk, where he publicly spoke out in favor of political pluralism (allowing opposition groups to coexist with the Communist party), human rights, and political freedom. In Gdansk, he met with Lech Walesa for a one-on-one conversation. The pope's visit rekindled support for Solidarity. At a time of apathy and pessimism, the pope's presence gave Poles new hope, and gave Lech Walesa renewed courage to continue his struggle in behalf of the Polish workers.

Although neither Poles nor the rest of the world knew it at the time, the most important turning point of all for Poland probably came two years earlier in the Soviet Union. When Mikhail Gorbachev took power in that country in March 1985, Solidarity was an illegal underground institution, banned from operating anywhere in the country.

Gorbachev gradually ushered in a program of economic and social reform known as *glasnost* (political openness and a new tolerance for diverse opinions) and *perestroika* (an economic restructuring of the country). He allowed and even encouraged the nations of East Central Europe to do the same. Walesa himself praised Gorbachev and said that he admired the way Gorbachev juggled so many important matters at the same time without losing his grip on any of them.[8] It was high praise for the man who was the first secretary of the Communist party of the Soviet Union. And it came from a man who had contributed so much to the downfall of Communism in Poland.

There is no way to know what would have become of Solidarity and its leader, Lech Walesa, without Gorbachev. But one thing was sure. The world would change dramatically in the Gorbachev years. And Lech Walesa and Poland would lead the way.

CHAPTER 8

SOLIDARITY REBORN

It is ironic that an ideology whose roots are that the workers will unite and rebel was overthrown by workers uniting and rebelling.[1]

SAM KAPLAN

In 1989 political changes in Poland set a precedent for the complete restructuring of East Central Europe. Lech Walesa engineered a compromise with the Polish government that led to the reinstitution of Solidarity as a legal organization. Soon after that, he also engineered a bloodless coup that for the first time in history placed a non-Communist government at the head of a Soviet satellite state. The Communist party of Poland lost its monopoly of power. Before long, other socialist countries within the Soviet bloc also ousted their Communist rulers, and Mikhail Gorbachev, head of the Soviet Union, did not use military force to prevent it.

The period leading up to and including these changes did not seem particularly promising for Poland. Massive demonstrations and strikes no longer occurred, and it seemed as if Solidarity's popular support had actually dwindled. Public support for Solidarity did not end, but it seemed to have gone into hiding, as if the people needed some time to gather their energy. Nevertheless, Solidarity was still the only active voice of political opposition with any real power in the society, and it continued to play a major role in political life. But Solidarity remained an outlawed institution, and Lech Walesa faced a long, hard fight to redeem its legal status. For the present, Solidarity existed only as an underground political organization and opposition movement.

THE ROUNDTABLE AGREEMENT

By 1988, voices of social opposition increasingly called for roundtable negotiations between the government and other groups. They wanted a dialogue in which everyone would have an equal place in the discussions (hence the round table). The Communist leadership would have to confer with university professors, scientists, other professionals, and former Solidarity leaders about how to solve Poland's pressing economic and social problems. After repeated refusals and delays, the government finally agreed to hold roundtable discussions in February 1989. Lech Walesa led the unofficial Solidarity delegation.

Why did the regime agree to hold roundtable discussions? Why were they willing to make such an incredible political compromise? The answer is simple: economics. The government's decision to recognize Solidarity as a discussion partner had a lot to do with the terrible economic crisis Poland faced. Productivity was very low. Inflation was unchecked and growing. It averaged over 100 percent in 1988 and became much worse in the beginning of 1989. A loaf of bread doubled in price in only a few short weeks. Many Poles felt that it was useless to try to save, because the money would be worth much less in the future. So they began to spend their money just as fast as they earned it, which served only to make whatever goods were available disappear that much more quickly. The result was even longer lines.

Heavy and prolonged investment was necessary to solve Poland's economic crisis. An inefficient technological base had to be replaced with a modern one. New and more efficient machines were necessary to increase production. Communication and transportation systems had to be modernized. Obsolete telephone systems had to be replaced. Cracow's central telephone system, for example, had been purchased from Sweden decades earlier; it was outdated and could not handle the demands of modern communication requirements. Rumor had it that the Swedes were so impressed that the system was still working that they wanted to buy it back and put it in a museum. The conclusion was obvious: an economic solution to Poland's problems would require immense investments. But where would the money come from?

Every economist knows that investment money comes from saving. And saving means not spending—not purchasing consumer goods and services. The money saved could go into building a society's economic base. In a capitalist society, saving and investment were done primarily by private business owners, or entrepreneurs, who reinvested part of their profits in new equipment (machinery, technology, and so on). In a socialist economy like Poland's, saving was done automatically by the state, which owned and ran the factories. Profits (whatever surplus the state had left over, after it paid itself, the workers, and the other costs of production) were automatically reinvested in new technology. But now the government needed a substantial increase in its rate of investment to solve Poland's economic problems. This could be accomplished in only two ways.

One way to increase investment was to borrow money from the West and use it to purchase Western technology. This was what the Gierek government did in the 1970s, and Poland had little to show for it. Bureaucratic waste and government mismanagement had squandered millions of dollars' worth of foreign loans. Foreign debt had reached a staggering $39 billion dollars by 1989. Poland could barely afford to meet the interest payments on these loans and was constantly in danger of defaulting on its repayment schedule. Western banks refused to lend Poland any more money, especially in the absence of harsh economic reforms.

The other way the state could get more money for investment was to pay the workers less or raise the prices of the goods it sold on the market. But this required an immediate and substantial lowering of the standard of living for the Polish people. In the words of Robert L. Heilbroner: "The saving necessary for investment can come from agriculture, manufacturing enterprises, and many other sources. In poor nations, it must also often be wrung from workers or peasants, by denying them the use of all the nation's economic potential to fill their consumption needs."[2]

Poles were asked to give up consumer goods in order to increase investment. They would have to suffer even more before things could get better. But there was little hope that the people would accept the harsh economic realities necessary to reform the system as long as they were carried out by a government that had never gained their trust. In the past, whenever the government had given the people that message, it had been met with strong social protests (see Chapter 3). The image of the "red bourgeoisie" was still haunting Poles. The leaders always asked the people to suffer while they themselves got rich. People recalled sarcastically how government spokesperson Jerzy Urban once had the poor judgment to state publicly that no matter how bad the economy got, the government would have no problem feeding itself.

In May and August of 1988 government economic policies produced another series of strikes in the Baltic coast shipyards and in the coal mines of Silesia. The result was predictable. The strikes were settled. These strikes did much to convince the government that negotiations with Solidarity were necessary. Remarkably, it was not the leaders of Solidarity who called the strikes, but a younger generation of Polish workers who did not require Solidarity's approval for their actions. This time the workers were not chanting "*Nie ma wolności, bez solidarności*" (There is no freedom without Solidarity) as they had in the past. Walesa had predicted as much. For years he had told the government that unless his moderate program was adopted, he would not be able to control the workers indefinitely and a terrible social upheaval might occur. The government could not risk introducing any new measures of economic austerity at this time. The danger of violent and massive social protest was too real.

However, if the government could bring the opposition (Solidarity) into the economic solution itself, major social protests might be avoided. If the government could get Solidarity to agree that the harsh economic measures it proposed were necessary, then perhaps the workers would not paralyze the country again by going on strike. This was why the government agreed to the roundtable discussions. This was why the government agreed to legalize Solidarity once again. It had little choice. The government could keep its political power by force, but it could not rule the country effectively. In the end it chose to strike a compromise with the opposition.

Lech Walesa and Solidarity's other leaders were willing to accept the harsh economic solution only if they were allowed to share power with the government. At the very least, they required a return of the legal status of the union and some increased democratization of the political system.

The government had another closely related but more practical reason for making these political concessions: it would no longer take all the blame if proposed solutions failed; Solidarity would share the responsibility for any drastic steps taken to reform the economy. Maybe then it would be not only a government leader who would be forced to resign in disgrace but also Lech Walesa, head of a trade union that had endorsed the reform program. Because of this, some of Solidarity's leaders were reluctant to accept the government's offer of a roundtable compromise. They wanted the union to remain on the sidelines and not get involved in the government's economic reforms. Walesa thought otherwise, and his decision proved a wise one, showing again his uncanny knack for seizing a political opportunity. Before the government's compromise with Solidarity was over, political power would shift entirely to the forces of Solidarity, and it would do so by completely legal, nonviolent means.

During the roundtable discussions Solidarity began to assert itself again. By the time the Roundtable Agreement was signed on April 5, 1989, the government had agreed to recognize the union and give it official status again. Even Rural Solidarity was granted legal status. Solidarity was also given the right of access to the news media. Besides regular television and radio broadcasts of opposition views, Solidarity was also allowed to set up and print a national daily newspaper, *Gazeta wyborcza* (Electoral Gazette) and a weekly, *Tygodnik Solidarność* (Solidarity Weekly). In exchange, Solidarity agreed to curb any future strikes that could cripple the nation when the government reform package was introduced. All in all, the agreement seemed like a huge political defeat for the Communist leadership. Eight years earlier the government had declared martial law to prevent just such a sharing of power with opposition forces. Now it was willing to give up through peaceful negotiations what it had so painfully gained.

The Roundtable Agreement did much more than just legalize Solidarity, although that alone was extremely significant. It also devised a new system of government based on the American, British, and French models. A new Polish constitution provided for a separation of powers, divided into three branches of government: legislative, executive, and judicial. It also set up a system of checks and balances similar to the one called for in the U.S. Constitution. Separate branches were to have veto power over the other branches, thus preventing any one branch from becoming too powerful. Solidarity's main purpose here was to prevent the return of any form of totalitarian government, Communist or otherwise, in the future.

Significantly for future developments, the new Polish Constitution created two chambers (or houses) within the legislative branch of government: the Senate and the Sejm (Parliament). The two chambers together formed the National Assembly, the equivalent of the U.S. Congress, which was to be responsible for making the laws of the land. It also created the office of president, the official head of the state and the commander in chief of the army. A prime minister was to set up and run the government. The prime minister's responsibility was to form a cabinet, composed of all the ministries (defense, finance, education, agriculture, interior, and so on), which would run the daily operation of the government. The president and the National Assembly had veto power over each other in the selection of prime minister.

The agreement worked out in the roundtable discussions was a compromise by which the Communist party and Solidarity would share a measure of power in the National Assembly. Free elections were to be held in the near future to elect all representatives to the Senate. The Sejm, on the other hand, would still be controlled by the Communist party. This ensured that the Party would not be excluded from power, no matter how it fared in the elections. Completely free elections to the Sejm were scheduled to take place three years later, in 1992. At that point Solidarity would be free to elect a majority in both chambers and thus gain control of the National Assembly. As it turned out, the country did not have to wait that long.

The Roundtable Agreement marked a tremendous turning point in postwar Polish history. No longer did the Communist party have a monopoly of power. A system based upon one-party dictatorship gave way to one based upon political pluralism, the sharing of power by various groups within the society. Walesa signed the Roundtable Agreement for Solidarity, while Czeslaw Kiszczak, minister of the interior, represented the government. Walesa said of the significance of the agreement: "For the first time, we accomplished something with the force of argument rather than the argument of force. . . . The agreements of the round table can become the beginning of the road to democracy."[3]

Completely free elections to the Senate were held in June 1989, another first for a Soviet bloc nation in the postwar period. In winning 99 out of the 100 seats in question, Solidarity representatives scored an amazing victory. The lone exception was a man who had run as an independent. The Communist party of Poland did not win a single seat. It was a humiliating defeat for its leaders. The Party had not expected to win the elections, but it had expected at least a small showing. Nevertheless, according to the terms of the Roundtable Agreement, the Communists still had 65 percent of the votes in the Sejm. They were able to elect their man, Wojciech Jaruzelski, president of Poland by a single vote in the National Assembly.

THE POWER SHIFT

Things continued to worsen for the regime. The Communist party in Poland was actually a combination of three related parties. The largest and most important was the PZPR, the Polish United Workers' Party. But there were also two smaller Communist parties: the United Peasants' party and the Democratic party. In the past, these parties had always acted as rubber stamps for the policies of the PZPR, behaving more like units of the PZPR than separate political parties.

It was here that Lech Walesa achieved perhaps his greatest political coup. He met privately with the leaders of these two parties. After coming to an agreement, Walesa and the two leaders of the parties came out on the street while Polish and Western news media filmed them. Walesa stood between the other two, hands tightly clasped and raised as a sign of victory. Walesa had just struck a political alliance that would ultimately break the back of the Communist party in Poland. When he persuaded these two smaller parties to vote on the side of Solidarity in the National Assembly, the PZPR no longer had a majority of votes. The PZPR could no longer choose the prime minister. The practical result of all this was that the PZPR no longer had the ability to form a government with itself at the head. The Communist government fell, and Walesa scored a tremendous political victory. Ironically, the Communists had helped in this process.

Why did the other two party leaders join Walesa? For one thing, they wanted to shed their image as puppet parties for the PZPR. They had just seen the results of the June elections, when the Communist parties had not won a single delegate, and they feared that they might be swept away in the next election. On the other hand, the head of the PZPR,

Wojciech Jaruzelski, still faced a dilemma. Should he, and perhaps more important, *could* he, allow Solidarity to take direct control of the government by allowing a non-Communist to become prime minister?

Under typical postwar circumstances, this was the time when the Communist party of the Soviet Union would have stepped in and told the Polish government to get its house in order. The message from Russia to Poland might have gone something like this: "Solidarity is threatening to start a counterrevolution against the Communist party. This must be stopped. Either you stop it yourselves or we will do it for you." This was probably the message sent by Brezhnev in 1981 that led to the declaration of martial law. But this was 1989, and the leader of the Soviet Union was Mikhail Gorbachev. Gorbachev was much more tolerant of political change than Brezhnev, and did not demand that the Polish leader force a Communist victory. As president, Jaruzelski still could have blocked a Solidarity-backed candidate, but that would have created a political stalemate, with no side able to form a government. In fact, it was reportedly Gorbachev himself who suggested to Jaruzelski during a phone conversation that he should agree to the formation of a Solidarity-led government.[4]

Walesa could have assumed the post of prime minister. The National Assembly even proposed his name for the position. But Walesa refused. He felt his role was to be leader of Solidarity, not head of the Polish government. Solidarity's victory brought to a head the crisis of identity that had plagued the organization from the moment of its creation. What *was* Solidarity? Was it a trade union focused on the economic interests of its members? Or was it a political party with its own political goals and with aspirations to power? In many ways it tried to be both. Eventually, this dual identity would contribute to a split in the Solidarity organization.

Walesa used his influence in the National Assembly to support Tadeusz Mazowiecki for prime minister. Mazowiecki—who, like Walesa, had been a political prisoner—was a strong Solidarity activist and former editor of the

Catholic journal *Więź*. Walesa had no official power in the government; he was making decisions and exerting his will on the force of his own charismatic personality as leader of a trade union with wide popular support. Communist party leader Jaruzelski, seeing that he was defeated, agreed to the nomination. On August 18, 1989, Mazowiecki became prime minister, the first non-Communist head of government in the Soviet bloc.

This event marked the beginning of the end of communism in East Central Europe. The non-Communist government immediately began a program of economic and social reform, and Poland was on its way to being transformed into a capitalist democracy. Within a few months the Communist party in Poland withered away and became a thing of the past. In 1989 the remaining countries of the Soviet bloc also overthrew their Communist regimes, and they did so in an even more abrupt manner. Instead of a gradual loss of power, large anti-Communist demonstrations and riots quickly overturned the other Communist governments of East Central Europe.

Western leaders had often used the analogy of falling dominoes to refer to capitalist countries succumbing in rapid succession to Communist revolutions in certain regions of the world. If one country fell to Communist control, then other neighboring countries would also fall. This "domino theory" was applied in particular to Southeast Asia during the Vietnam War. Ironically, however, it was the Communist countries of East Central Europe that now fell like dominoes from Communist control. Once Gorbachev had unleashed the forces of social change, there was no way for him to stop them or even to limit their scope. Communism in East Central Europe was rapidly crumbling, and Lech Walesa and his fellow Poles had led the way.

THE ROLE OF INTERNATIONAL POLITICS

Who was the person most responsible for the death of communism in East Central Europe? Many would answer that question with the name Lech Walesa. But others would fill in the name Mikhail Gorbachev.[5] Although it's true that without Gorbachev, Poland and the other Soviet bloc nations would have had a very different history, it was Walesa who started the trend in 1980. Gorbachev did not arrive on the scene until 1985. And Gorbachev's intention was not to overthrow communism but to reform it. He remained a loyal member of the Communist party. Walesa's goal was to bring down the entire system, as we'll see in Chapter 9. Still, there can be no doubt that much of the success of the social protest movement in East Central Europe was made possible by the reforms of Mikhail Gorbachev, who served as head of the Soviet Union until December 25, 1991.

Polish history and the ultimate success of the Solidarity movement cannot be understood without considering the complex political relationships among the superpowers. Those relationships provided a backdrop to change in Poland. There was a clear link between internal developments in Poland and world politics. Poland's geographical location has always left it vulnerable to political manipulation by foreign powers. Historically, this has been mostly to the detriment of Poland.

Poland had often been a point of conflict between the United States and the Soviet Union. The United States strongly protested Stalin's incorporation of East Central Europe into its political orbit at the end of World War II. Throughout the postwar period, the Soviet Union did what was necessary, including the use of military force, to ensure that these countries stayed there. This policy became known as the Brezhnev Doctrine, and it was applied in the Prague Spring of 1968. An earlier version was applied during the Hungarian uprising of 1956. In both instances the Red Army invaded the rebellious neighbors and brought them back into line with Moscow's wishes. Twice Poland had come close to the same fate. Once in 1956, when Gomulka returned to power, and again in 1980 and 1981, when Solidarity threatened Soviet domination of Poland.

But in 1989 the situation was radically different. By now international politics had created the climate for Poland's independence as a free nation of Europe. Gorbachev openly modified the Brezhnev Doctrine. His programs, *glasnost* and *perestroika*, were not compatible with a show of military force. In the end, Gorbachev was willing to let the countries of East Central Europe go their own way even if that meant they would reject socialism. He would not send in the Red Army to crush the breakaway nations. As we have seen, Gorbachev even recommended that a Solidarity-led government in Poland be established in August 1989.

Gorbachev's rise to power in the Soviet Union had far-reaching consequences for the future development of Poland. When martial law was declared in 1981, Brezhnev was the head of the USSR. The changes that took place in Poland and the rest of East Central Europe in 1989 would probably not have occurred if Leonid Brezhnev had still been in power.

THE RETURN OF CAPITALISM

The fall of the Communist party in Poland was also accompanied by a rejection of the symbols of Soviet rule. Street names were one example. Many streets had been named after prominent Communist leaders and important events in Soviet history. Poles now demanded the restoration of their former names. Names like Stalingrad's Heroes Street and July Manifesto Street were quickly changed to Piłsudski Street or Kosciuszko Street. Both of these heroes of Polish history stood up to the Russians militarily (see Chapter 1). In one case, July 22nd Street (marking the day in 1944 when the Soviet-backed Lublin government of Poland officially declared its power) was changed to May 3rd Street (referring to the drafting of the Polish liberal constitution on May 3, 1791).

Another example was the removal of monuments and statues of famous Soviet heroes such as Lenin, the Russian revolutionary who adapted Marxism to the Russian Revolution of 1917, and Feliks Dzerzhinski, the Pole who became the first head of Lenin's secret police. These statues were taken down amid huge crowds that had gathered to enjoy the ceremony of the fall of Soviet-sponsored Communist rule.

The Mazowiecki government now set out to reform the economy by bringing capitalism back to Poland. No one knew if the economic experiment would work. It had never been done before. No economic system had ever gone from a socialist economy to a capitalist economy. Solidarity brought in advisers to introduce capitalist economic policies. Some economists even came from the West. It was decided that a program of rapid transition to capitalism was better than a go-slow approach, which would only prolong the inevitable pain. Since the economic program was to bring capitalism to Poland very quickly, it was sometimes referred to as a policy of economic shock therapy.

The finance minister of Poland, Leszek Balcerowicz, was a key figure in the government's economic reform package. He immediately attacked the problem of inflation, which had skyrocketed to an annual rate of over 1,000 percent in 1989. One writer reported the changes this way: "The government imposed an immediate and total pay freeze, limiting domestic purchasing power. Thus previous shortages of consumer goods were eliminated, although the value of real wages dropped by 40 percent."[6] Since people now had less money with which to buy goods, prices did not rise so fast, and inflation was brought under control by the summer of 1990.

Balcerowicz's economic program also focused on the problem of production. Under the socialist system, industry had been owned by the state. Now a way had to be found to return this industry to private ownership, the cornerstone of any capitalist economy. A privatization program was set up to transfer state-owned industries back into private hands. This program was combined with other economic reforms, such as allowing more individual buying and selling of goods, especially food products, and changing the laws to encourage foreign investment. Making the zloty, Poland's currency, readily transferable into the dollar and other Western currencies also helped to stimulate foreign investment in Poland.

These programs were largely successful in bringing Poland rapidly into the ranks of the capitalist nations of the world. It was more profitable now for farmers to sell their products on the free market, so the supply of goods available to the public dramatically increased, and the long lines at the food stores soon disappeared. But many problems still remained. For one thing, consumer goods remained so expensive that most Poles simply could not afford to buy them. Under socialism, a main problem had been the lack of goods in the stores. Under capitalism, there were now many goods on the shelves but very little money with which to buy them. Capitalism had come to Poland, but it was not what most Poles had expected.

Another problem created by the capitalist reforms was unemployment. Since the state no longer guaranteed jobs, as it had under socialism, many people were thrown out of work by the new economic policies. Although Poles in general were very pleased that socialism was gone, they now experienced some of the negative effects of its absence. One thing that socialism had provided was a relatively secure social safety net, which prevented people from actually starving. There were also very few homeless people in socialist Poland. (PZPR spokesperson Jerzy Urban had even sarcastically called on Poles to collect blankets for the homeless and have them shipped to New York City.) Maybe their old socialist jobs did not pay them much, but at least they had jobs. Poles had often joked in the past that there was little incentive to work in the state-owned factories: "Whether we work hard or lie down on the job, we still get paid the same measly salary." But now the lack of job security was a major fear. Although the new Polish government quickly passed an unemployment bill to ease the transition, many people still longed for a safe and secure job. Not knowing where the next paycheck was coming from was something Poles had not experienced under communism, and it was unnerving.

For the first time since World War II, a stock exchange opened in Poland in the spring of 1991. Ironically it occupied the former headquarters of the Polish Communist party. This shocking turn of events was in a way symbolic of all that had happened to Poland since 1980. Capitalism had replaced communism as part of the economic reforms. And in fact, the word "reform" was no longer appropriate. The centralized economic system under the Communist party was not reformed; it was replaced altogether. Poland jumped full speed ahead into a free market economy. It was a tremendous risk to try to overhaul the economic system so radically. Much economic suffering was created in the process. But for a while at least, the people were much more willing to accept that suffering. At least it meant that their government was now making the reforms.

Although the new economic policy was referred to as shock therapy, in the long run Mazowiecki proved to be moderate in his approach to solving the problems of the country. Walesa himself, astutely sensing the mood of the nation, preferred an even more radical program. He decided to run for president in 1990. In doing so, he caused a major division in the Solidarity union. He ran against his former friend and Solidarity activist, Tadeusz Mazowiecki, who was still prime minister. Support from Solidarity was thus divided between these two men, and Solidarity split into two factions, and then into many different political parties.

Many Poles felt that Walesa should not run for president. He had been superb as the leader of a labor union and as a political activist fighting Communist policies. But now he was entering an arena in which he had no real experience. Couldn't Walesa better serve the nation as an elder statesman who could remind the new government of its true duties, but not get involved in day-to-day politics?

I was able to interview Lech Walesa in Gdansk in August, 1990, just prior to his decision to run for president.

CHAPTER 9

AN INTERVIEW WITH LECH WALESA

Why am I successful? Very simple. Because I speak the truth. I do not speculate. . . . I have no strengths other than that of the heart and my faith.[1]

LECH WALESA

Walesa's Solidarity office at the Gdansk headquarters was located about one block from the main gate of the Lenin shipyard. As I walked into his office in anticipation of my interview, I noticed a huge picture above his desk. Walesa was sitting at his desk, head down, writing a memo. But I could not help staring at the picture. It was a collage of three images superimposed on a red background: the Polish eagle, the Black Madonna, and the Solidarity logo. These three images symbolized the three main institutions of Polish society after 1980: the Polish state, the Catholic church, and the free trade union. Before World War II the Polish eagle was always portrayed with a crown on its head, but the Communist party leaders removed the crown after the war. They felt that the new, Communist phase of Polish history made the crown obsolete. The Polish eagle without the crown soon became the symbol of Communist Poland. The Polish eagle in Walesa's office was wearing its crown again.

Walesa the strike leader is a man of action, not words. "I am not a historian or a theoretician," he said. "I am interested only in the truth." He easily becomes impatient with endless theoretical discussions and lectures. He does not feel as comfortable in a private interview about himself as he does in a knock-down-drag-out debate with his political opponents.

Walesa is not known for his speaking eloquence. As he himself admitted in his autobiography, "Previously, I always spoke faster than I could think, and my speeches were often a flop as a result: I would start off well, the argument would be a good one, but then, gradually, I would lose the thread of what I was saying."[2]

Walesa does not like to waste time, but prefers to get down to business immediately. He does not mince words; he says what is on his mind and his listener can take it or leave it. But the words he speaks are honest and from the heart; he is not hypocritical. Walesa attributes the tremendous support given to him by the people, at least in part, to this quality.

I knew of this aspect of Walesa's personality from general press reports and from my personal discussions with Polish citizens. It did not take long for me to personally experience it at my first meeting with him in the summer of 1990.[3] Solidarity's second in charge, Stefan Jurczak, had arranged the interview and introduced me to Walesa in his office. I had barely finished our handshake and "I am very pleased to meet you, sir," when Walesa broke in and told me not to waste time talking about who I was and what I was doing in Poland. "In urging me to grant you this interview, Stefan filled me in on all that," he said. "So let's get right down to business. What can I do for you? What do you want to know from me? I'm sorry to be so abrupt, but we don't have that much time. Later this morning I have a meeting with two U.S. senators, and I don't want to have to cut our interview short without getting to all your main questions. I'm sorry, would you like to sit down on the couch over there? There's a table you can write on. Would you like some coffee?" His mind was obviously racing a mile a minute, and he changed subjects faster than I could keep up with him.

His long years of political activism had also conditioned him to be suspicious of people and curious about their motives. Very early in the interview, despite his prior comment about not talking about me, he asked me about the book I was writing. He was particularly interested to know just who had given me the offer to write such a book: "Who will be the publisher of this book? What type of a book will it be? To whom will the book be targeted?"

I showed him a copy of Michael Kort's biography of Nikita Khrushchev, leader of the Communist party of the Soviet Union at the height of the Cold War from 1953 to 1964. That book is from the same series as this one.[4] Khrushchev was perhaps best known in America for having backed down during the Cuban missile crisis in October 1962 and for his visit to the United States in 1959. During that visit, he took off his shoe at the United Nations and banged it on a table. It was Khrushchev who said, "We will bury you," by which he meant that communism would ultimately be victorious over capitalism. I smiled at Walesa as I handed him the book, realizing that he fully sensed the irony of the situation. (Not only did Khrushchev's prediction not come true, but I was now talking to the man who, perhaps more than any other single individual, was responsible for the downfall of communism in East Central Europe.) I jokingly remarked: "I'm sorry to include you in such company, but this is an example of the type of book I will be writing." He laughed out loud for the first and only time during our interview, and then suddenly became serious again: "No need to apologize. Khrushchev was a very important historical figure who deserves to have many books written about him."

The Western press has sometimes depicted Lech Walesa as a shipyard electrician who "got mad" when the government raised meat prices, and led his fellow workers to a strike that ultimately brought down the government. Walesa is depicted as a simple and somewhat naive worker who had no idea that his local strike would lead to a full-blown social upheaval. In this view, Walesa is sometimes compared to Martin Luther, the monk who started the Protestant Reformation. In 1517 Luther began his protest against corrupt Catholic church practices, never dreaming that his actions would lead to a complete breakdown of the unity of the church. Others compare Walesa to Mikhail Gorbachev, who was overwhelmed when his reforms grew beyond his control into a major social upheaval that ultimately destroyed a system he had no desire to destroy in the first place.

These are not valid analogies. Walesa should be seen as a clever political activist whose goal from the start was, at the very least, to radically reform the entire economic system of Poland. His willingness to endure setback after setback, both personal and political, in order to achieve his goal was forged by long-standing activism combined with deep religious faith. The abolition of the entire political and economic system of Polish communism was always in the back of his mind. Perhaps he would not see that day himself, perhaps he would have to settle for many compromises along the way, but his ultimate goal was still one of radical social change. Although he was pleasantly surprised by the speed of the actual turn of events, he was not overwhelmed or shocked that they had occurred. It was as if he could now turn to his fellow Poles and say, "I knew it! I knew that the Communist system couldn't last."

"My goal from the start," he told me, "was to bring down the entire Communist system in Poland."

This was the statement that shocked me the most during the interview. I remembered Walesa as a man of moderation, a man of compromise, not a radical social revolutionary trying to bring down the Communist system. I had lived in Cracow from 1976 to 1982, so I was basing this conclusion on my personal experience. More than once I had heard Walesa state publicly that Solidarity was "not against socialism, but for a better, more just form of socialism."

I challenged his comment with a look of disbelief, which

he immediately addressed: "Of course, I couldn't say that at the time. I couldn't say that our real goal was to throw out the Communists. That would have been fatal to any hope of success. At the very least, I would have been arrested immediately, and they would have thrown away the key. So I had to go slowly. I had to compromise. I had to pretend that I only wanted to bring a measure of justice and reform to the Communist system, not abolish it completely."

If Walesa was telling me the truth, and I believe that he was, his words illustrate his tremendous political realism. Why do I believe Walesa was telling me the truth? For the six years that I lived in Poland, I heard that same "secret" wish from hundreds, if not thousands, of Poles. That was really no surprise. What really shocked me about Walesa's comment was that, given the political reality of the time, he actually believed it could be accomplished. And he was going to work tirelessly toward that end. Once again, what the West would have called naive and unfounded optimism turned out to be keen political perception. Western scholars and political analysts were wrong; an electrician from the Gdansk shipyards was right. But Walesa had the upper hand in the analysis. He knew and understood popular sentiment in Poland better than they did. He was part of it.

"Were you surprised by your success?" I asked him. "Not at all," he replied. "I was more surprised that the Communist system lasted as long as it did, given the fact that so much of the society was against it. You know, you must realize that the intense criticism and hatred of the Communist system in Poland was widespread among all aspects of Polish society. It was not just the workers who were fed up with the Communist party. You could also find many members of the police and the state bureaucracy who felt the same way. Even members of the Communist party themselves had become disenchanted with the system. Looking back, ninety-nine percent of the society was against the system. How could it possibly have held together indefinitely? It's a miracle it held together as long as it did. The government policies did terrible harm to the country. Just look at the ecological damage alone. They really ruined the country in many ways. The Communists had to go. The only question that really remained was how long it would take."

Another example of Walesa's self-confidence and pride can be seen when he spoke of his internment period after his arrest following the declaration of martial law on December 13, 1981. At that time he defiantly proclaimed: "Now I know that I have won the struggle and they have lost. Someday they will come to me on their knees, begging *me* to help save the situation." When Walesa spoke these words, he had no idea when or if he would be released from prison, or even if he faced a worse fate.

Reflecting on his last statement, Walesa turned to me and smiled slightly: "Well, I guess maybe I exaggerated then. Maybe I shouldn't have said that at the time. Maybe it was too bold, too arrogant. But as it turned out, I *was* right. The essence of what I meant by those words did in fact come true. Force alone cannot control a society indefinitely. At that particular moment I felt that the Communist system in Poland was doomed." At the darkest moment in Solidarity's history, when it appeared that the movement would be snuffed out of existence and all the previous gains would be lost, Walesa remained totally committed to his cause and extremely optimistic about the long-term future.

Walesa spoke almost tenderly of the changes that had been taking place in Poland in 1980 and 1981 when Solidarity was first recognized as a legal trade union. He repeatedly used the word "evolution" to describe these changes. By this, he explained, he meant that the demands of the Solidarity movement had to be kept to a minimum at first. Only gradually, with the passage of time, could they be expanded. However, he did not mean that the core of the demands would change, or evolve, into something else. He simply meant that Solidarity's program for change could not be fully disclosed all at once. Part of that program had to be kept in the background; the government would never have allowed it. The whole movement might have been prematurely crushed. Solidarity's leaders would have been arrested, put on trial for anti-state, anti-socialist, and counterrevolutionary behavior, and sentenced to long prison terms. Walesa's approach proved that he was a shrewd political opponent, not a naive idealist. "We would talk to the government about economic issues and then, little by little, very softly, begin to change the topic to freedom."

As long as the demands were limited and focused on politically nonthreatening issues such as consumer demands, the government could not accuse Solidarity of anti-socialist activities. In 1980–1981 Walesa often went out of his way to emphasize that neither he nor Solidarity was anti-socialist. Rather, he stated repeatedly that Solidarity only wanted a better socialism, a socialism that was more responsive to the needs of the people. How could the Communist party object to that? When addressing the workers, Walesa was honest and forthcoming. When making public statements that he knew both the Polish authorities and the Soviet Union's security apparatus were carefully monitoring, Walesa became a political pragmatist. Honesty was one thing; stupidity leading to political suicide was quite another.

He was almost apologetic in addressing this last topic. He did not want to give me the impression that he had caved in to political pressures because of fear of governmental retaliation. "Concessions were absolutely necessary. We had to accept socialism if we were to have any real chance of success. As it was, we were taking a giant step forward at the time. Later, we would be able to take other, more radical steps. But not then. In order to get anywhere at all, we had to go slowly and make concessions." Again, nonviolent evolution was preferable to a potentially bloody all-out confrontation with the government.

I asked him about the development in Poland of a multiparty system rather than a two-party system like the one in the United States. "Americans do not understand why we are developing many different political parties. They think we should have only two. They don't understand why it is necessary at this stage of development in Poland to have political pluralism. We fought very long and hard for political freedom. We need to show how that freedom is reflected in the political system. If that freedom means being willing to endure the inconveniences and inefficiencies of a multiparty system, then so be it. It is more important that we demonstrate the fruits of political freedom by allowing a multiparty system than it is to adopt a more practical two-party system."

Many Poles are still unhappy about Walesa's position on this and related points. Moreover, they feel that Walesa himself was largely responsible for the splitting up of Solidarity into many different factions. As far back as 1980, after the initial success of Solidarity, Walesa felt that a multiparty system was inevitable, and therefore he did not try to stop it in 1990. He could have used his tremendous influence to prevent this from happening, but Solidarity had to stand united in its opposition to the Communist government. On this point Walesa was adamant. But once victory was achieved, he did not see the splitting up of Solidarity supporters into separate factions as necessarily a bad thing.

And what of the situation in 1990? When asked about his differences of opinion with other former Solidarity leaders, he replied, "You know, some of my colleagues want to stop and rest on the recent gains that we have made. They want to go slowly; I want to go fast. I fight with them constantly on this issue. I want more radical change."

While the Communist authorities were in power, and until the threat of Soviet invasion was completely eliminated, Walesa's radical instincts were tempered by political necessity. Although he was a radical reformer, he knew when it was time to back down and go slowly and when it was time to stand up to the government and say, "We will not budge on this point." Now that victory was finally theirs and communism in Poland had been overcome, there was no longer any need for moderation. "The people do not want to wait for years for gradual results," he told me. "They want quick action now, not more promises."

This ability to perceive what the common Pole was thinking was, and is, Walesa's greatest asset. It was this platform for more radical change that won him the election for the presidency of Poland in December 1990. Once again he told the people what the majority wanted to hear: that capitalist reforms must proceed more quickly. This was also what he wanted.

While at the Solidarity headquarters in Gdansk, I met Walesa's personal secretaries and discussed with them what it was like to work for Walesa. This meeting took place entirely by chance. Knowing the acute shortage of such consumer items as coffee and chocolate, I had brought a modest supply of each as a thank-you gift for Stefan Jurczak and his staff. Somewhat embarrassed, Jurczak tried to refuse them, but after some persistence on my part, he finally proclaimed, "Okay, we'll have a small party for our American guest." Then he invited five or six of Walesa's personal secretaries to join us in his office for a coffee break.

The coffee break turned into an hour-long party. On Jurczak's office wall was a caricature of Walesa, depicted as a king sitting on the Polish throne. The running joke in Poland at the time was that Walesa was becoming too arrogant, "too big for his own britches"; perhaps he even wanted to restore the Polish monarchy with himself as the new king. One of the secretaries responded laughingly to my inquiry, "Yes, there may be a little truth to that caricature. Sometimes I think he does act as if he thinks he is the new king of Poland."

Then Jurczak addressed the secretaries: "Most of you have been working for Lech for quite some time. You all know him pretty well. Tell our guest from America what you really think of Lech Walesa. What is he really like? Don't be shy. Tell him the truth." The secretaries gazed at one another in uncertainty for a few seconds. Then one of them said, "Okay, why not be totally honest? After all, isn't that what Solidarity is all about? I'll tell you. We all love him very much. We all know and appreciate everything he has done not only for us but for our whole country. That goes without saying. But sometimes I'd like to wring his damn neck. He can irritate the hell out of me. He can be so demanding, so picky, so impatient, so arrogant, so lacking in understanding for what we as secretaries have to go through. Sometimes he just drives me crazy."

The others quickly agreed. He had won their love and admiration as a political activist and leader of Solidarity, but he had not yet learned, in their opinion, how to be a kind and understanding boss.

Jurczak later added his own assessment. "You know, I have worked with Walesa for many years now. I lived through the darkest periods when it seemed that all hope was gone. During this entire period I have seen Walesa make many important decisions crucial to the success of our movement, decisions that could have brought Solidarity to the brink of disaster had they turned out to be wrong. I have seen him many times forced to make such a decision in a matter of minutes, with no time for thoughtful consideration or discussion. And do you know that in all that time I have never once seen him make an important decision that later turned out to be a mistake—even though at the time I may have disagreed with him myself. The man is absolutely incredible. His skill for perceiving and subsequently avoiding political pitfalls is unsurpassed in our organization. Not only that, but the man simply remembers everything, every meeting he had with someone, what was discussed at the time, everything. His mind is incredibly quick. Perhaps it is this feature that makes him impatient with others whose mental powers are not as sharp. Some people may indeed perceive this as arrogance. But the fact that Walesa is the head of Solidarity is by no means a lucky quirk of fate. He truly deserves the recognition he has received."

CHAPTER 10

PRESIDENT WALESA AND THE FUTURE OF POLAND

The story of Poland is a story of hope, against all the odds.[1]

NEAL ASCHERSON

The significance of developments in Poland was apparent to the rest of the world during all stages of Poland's resistance to Soviet domination. Poland had achieved a number of firsts in the postwar era. It was the first and only country in the Soviet bloc in which the church was truly independent of the Communist authorities. Poland also had the distinction of having one of its native sons chosen as the spiritual leader of the Catholic church. It was the first country in the Soviet bloc where worker opposition toppled the Communist party leadership and brought down the government. It was the first country in the Soviet bloc to have a truly independent trade union for its workers, free from political control by the Communist party. And it was the first country in the Soviet bloc to have a non-Communist as the head of government.

On December 9, 1990, Lech Walesa was elected president by the Polish people in the first direct presidential elections in Poland's history. Two days after the elections, Walesa visited the shrine at Czestochowa, home of the Black Madonna. There he publicly proclaimed his first oath as president-elect of the Polish nation: "I swear steadfastly to defend the nation's dignity and the state's sovereignty and security."[2] Poland had at last achieved full political independence from the Soviet Union, and forty-five years of Communist rule had come to an end.

The story of Lech Walesa and the Solidarity movement can be viewed as an expression of the Polish struggle for national freedom. As such, Lech Walesa's personal struggle is very much in keeping with Polish tradition. Despite all the adversity and hardship, it is the story of optimism and hope for an independent Poland. There was a little romanticism present in Solidarity's roots, along with a deep-seated religious faith. At the time of Solidarity's birth in 1980, people like Lech Walesa, who believed that the moral force of society would ultimately prevail over the reality of tanks and bullets, were often considered naive idealists or hopeless dreamers. Even now, after the fall of communism in East Central Europe, it seems odd to write that the unarmed workers of Poland could be an even match for the military potential of the Moscow-backed Polish regime. Yet history has shown that this was the case.

Of the three major institutions of Polish society in the 1980s, two of them, the Catholic church and Solidarity, were united in their opposition to the third, the Communist party. The Party was thus outnumbered two to one. And Lech Walesa scored a major political victory in 1980 when his union was granted legal status. But as long as the Communist party's political alliance with the Soviet Union was intact, the odds were really two to two. In December 1981, the Communist party temporarily got the upper hand again when it outlawed the Solidarity trade union, arrested hundreds of its leaders, and declared a national state of emergency.

But by 1989 the voices of moral protest had resurfaced, and when events in the Soviet Union allowed it, they finally prevailed. After a landslide victory in the June 1989 elections, Solidarity soon found itself running the country. It seemed unbelievable, even to the members of Solidarity. One Solidarity activist, Henryk Wujec, described it as a time when "virtually straight from prison, we find ourselves in the palaces of power."[3] Who would have believed that political dissident Adam Michnik, as an editor of a legal Polish newspaper, would be allowed to write that "a specter is haunting Europe," the specter of democratization?[4] (Over one hundred forty years earlier Marx had declared that communism was that specter.) And who would have believed that Jacek Kuron, the often arrested leader of KOR and Poland's most famous political dissident, would become minister of labor?

By 1990 Lech Walesa, the former shipyard electrician, was running for president of Poland in a free and democratic election. Neither of his rival candidates belonged to the Communist party. One was Stanislaw Tyminski, a successful businessman of Polish descent who had lived in Canada for many years and had come back to Poland to run for president. The other was Tadeusz Mazowiecki, a Solidarity activist whom Walesa had helped become prime minister only a few months before. On December 9, 1990, Walesa won a second round of runoff elections with approximately 75 percent of the votes. The blacklisted political activist who could not find a job was now president of his country. All this, too, had seemed completely impossible just a few years before.

Walesa's formal inauguration took place in Warsaw on December 22, 1990. Promising never to forget his peasant and worker roots, he said that his rise to the presidency should encourage other workers and farmers to feel responsible for their country. He warned that state officials should not count on enjoying public support indefinitely.[5] They had to earn it constantly. He proclaimed the establishment of the Third Republic of Poland. Later that day Walesa received a formal delegation of the Polish government-in-exile. During the entire postwar period, this government-in-exile had refused to recognize the Communist puppet government of the Soviet Union. For all these years, it had preserved the prewar Polish insignia and presidential seal abroad. Now its delegates were returning it to Poland to formally acknowledge the legitimacy of Lech Walesa as the democratically elected president of Poland.

WALESA'S PROGRAM FOR THE FUTURE

On the economic front, Walesa promised to continue the general policies of Balcerowicz, then deputy prime minister, as the best way to proceed. However, there would be certain modifications. First, privatization was to occur at an even quicker pace than before, and the government would make a greater effort to involve free and open public participation in the process. Second, decentralization of the state administration would also take place much faster. In the past, the central ministries in the capital had determined all important decisions. Now local managers and officials would have more say over what went on in their own areas, without having to get Warsaw's approval for every decision they made. These changes would allow a much faster transition to capitalism.

Other aspects of Walesa's new program included the following:

1. Fully democratic elections to Parliament, which still had some Communist members in it from the 1989 Roundtable Agreement.

2. The removal of the old Communist bureaucracy from management positions. Many of these people owed their positions to political connections or party membership, but there would be no witch-hunt of Communists; the new government would not resort to using the old methods of the Communists. Party members soon found themselves unemployed. Many wound up becoming taxi drivers. Poles joked that since most of them had big cars and few skills, driving a taxi was the logical choice of a new occupation.

3. The depoliticizing of the armed services. Politics

would be taken out of the army. As president, Walesa was commander in chief of the armed services. In the past, the army had been a tool of the Communist party. Now the army was to remain the prime instrument of national defense; it was not to get involved in supporting specific political groups.

4. Church and state would remain separate institutions.

This last point raised many questions in the minds of Polish dissidents and the general public. Many Poles felt that Walesa's close connections with the Catholic church threatened the independent actions of the government. Would Walesa allow the church to dictate state policy? Religious instruction in school and abortion were two issues that divided Poles. Some Poles even felt the church might become a hidden party that could run the government from behind the scenes, much as the Communist party had done in the past. Even though Walesa strongly denied these accusations, many doubts lingered.

Financial aid from the West was also important to Walesa's modernization program. This would lessen the suffering of the Polish people. The effect of international affairs on Poland's internal development was still painfully obvious to the government. Poland needed financial aid to ease it out of its economic crisis. Walesa and Solidarity had the political support of the West and thus were able to obtain at least some economic aid, including the restructuring of the debt payments.

Walesa's personal relationships with Americans and his feelings toward the United States also played a role in determining his economic policies. Walesa often looked to the American system to provide a model for future Polish development. His trip to the United States in 1989 underscored this point when he declared to a joint session of Congress that Poles would endeavor to build "a second America in Poland." Poles have always had strong ties to the United States and have looked to it as both an ally and a supporter. The large Polish-American community in the United States has also played a significant role in this regard, providing both financial and moral support.

After the official inauguration ceremonies were over, Poles began to sing. Besides the national anthem, they sang two other songs. One was *Sto lat, sto lat, niech żyje, żyje, nam* ("One hundred years, one hundred years, may he live a hundred years"). This is the Polish equivalent of "For He's a Jolly Good Fellow," which Poles sing on festive occasions and especially to honored guests such as the pope or U.S. presidents. Now they sang it to Lech Walesa, president of Poland. They also sang *Żeby Polską była Polską* ("Let Poland Be Poland"), a favorite song of the striking workers of Solidarity. It seemed as if the words they sang had now come true. Poland's freedom had finally been won, and Poland could simply be Poland once more.

An evaluation of Walesa's performance as president of Poland is a very difficult matter. Most Poles have not been kind or patient in evaluating his performance during the first few years of his presidency. They cite his frequent verbal gaffes—Walesa was never known for eloquent or sophisticated public speaking, but rather for his down-to-earth, emotional appeals—and what seems to many Poles to be the inadequacy of his policy implementations. Despite his calls for radical change, the privatization program in Poland is proceeding rather slowly. His policies have drawn strong protests from farmers, miners, and trade unionists, and painful price increases were implemented on January 1, 1990.

In fairness to Walesa, however, privatization of state-owned industries has proven to be a complicated and sensitive issue. The main concern is how to distribute property fairly, so that one group does not get too wealthy at the expense of the remaining population. Another concern is to find a way to privatize that does not lead to greater unemployment, with factory workers being forced out by the closing of inefficient plants. High unemployment remains the number one economic problem facing Poland today.

However, the most serious general attack Walesa faces is usually phrased something like this: "Walesa achieved a great deal as leader of the Solidarity trade union, and we all respect him for it. But he should have stopped there. He is not a politician: he does not understand all the workings of government, and he is making a difficult situation even worse." Adding to the force of the attacks is the appearance of scandals in the noncommunist Polish government. Many poles have become disillusioned with the process of democratization, saying that the new government is as corrupt as the former communist one. The victory of the socialist-oriented parties (the Democratic Left Alliance and the Peasant Party) in the parliamentary election of September 1993 was an example of this disillusionment with the pace of reform. The election was a setback for both Solidarity and the Catholic Church. Although few Poles actually want a return to the former system, the situation is troubling. The transition to capitalism is causing great suffering among many segments of the population, particularly the Polish farmers, who have been hard hit by the "shock therapy" tactics of the economic reforms. A Western observer offers a bleak summary of the situation:

> **For most Poles this "success" [of the shock therapy] means an uncertain future, with unemployment at 15 percent and rising; is has meant a drastic drop in living standards, the dramatic erosion of old-age pensions, a collapse in public health, education and other social services. It spells greed, growing inequality, the ruthless rule of money. For the few it is splendid, but the many have the vote.[6]**

In short, the road to capitalism and democracy has not turned out to be an easy one to travel. The present situation has created many new challenges for Lech Walesa. Whether he will be able to meet these challenges—as he has met many challenges in the past—remains an open question.

SOURCE NOTES

CHAPTER ONE

1. Lawrence Weschler, "A Reporter at Large (Poland—Part I)," *The New Yorker*, April 11, 1983, p. 73.

2. Henryk Sienkiewicz, *The Deluge* (Boston: Little, Brown, 1925), vol. 2, pp. 3–4.

3. Actually the British constitution is the oldest, but it was, and is, unwritten.

4. Stefan Krzysztof Kuczynski, "The National Emblem, Colours, Anthem," in *Poland: The Country and Its People* (Warsaw: Interpress, 1979), p. 35.

5. Joseph Strayer et al., *The Course of Civilization* (New York: Harcourt, Brace & World, 1961), vol. 2, p. 441.

6. Stewart Steven, *The Poles* (New York: Macmillan, 1982), p. 278.

7. This issue has been hotly disputed by historians. It has also led to an emotionally charged debate within Poland itself.

8. The exact number is hard to determine, in large measure because of the dislocations of war.

CHAPTER TWO

1. Michael Kort, *The Soviet Colossus: A History of the USSR* (Boston: Unwin Hyman, 1990), p. 219.

2. Private agriculture also predominated in socialist Yugoslavia, but its geographical location and Yugoslav president Tito's skillful diplomacy

removed that country from the direct control of Moscow. As such, it was usually treated separately from other parts of East Central Europe belonging to the Soviet bloc.

3. Wladyslaw Kwasniewicz, personal communication, Cracow, 1976.

4. Kwasniewicz, 1976.

CHAPTER THREE

1. Warsaw wits, quoted by Daniel Singer, *The Road to Gdansk* (New York: Monthly Review Press, 1981), p. 212.

2. Jule Gatter-Klenk, *Gesprache mit Lech Walesa* (Konigstein/Ts: Athenaum, 1981), p. 45.

3. Neal Ascherson, *The Struggles for Poland* (New York: Random House 1987), p. 161.

4. Flora Lewis, *A Case History of Hope* (New York: Doubleday, 1958), p. 142.

5. Quoted in Lewis, p. 144.

6. Singer, p. 159.

7. Quoted in Alexander Niczow, *Black Book of Polish Censorship* (South Bend, Ind.: And Books, 1982), p. 38.

8. Niczow, p. 38.

9. Singer, p. 164.

10. Andrzej Korbonski, "Poland," in *Communism in Eastern Europe*, ed. T. Rakowska-Harmstone and A. Gyorgy (Bloomington: Indiana University Press, 1979), p. 47.

11. The name that the Solidarity underground was to take after martial law had outlawed their legal activities, the Temporary Coordinating Committee (TKK), later proved to be very appropriate.

12. Quoted in Gatter-Klenk, p. 45.

13. Quoted in Gatter-Klenk, p. 45.

14. Singer, pp. 171–72.

15. Quoted in Robert Eringer, *Strike for Freedom* (New York: Dodd, Mead, 1982), p. 31.

CHAPTER FOUR

1. Lech Walesa in a speech before the Italian Labour Conference, Geneva, June 5, 1981. Quoted in Denis MacShane, *Solidarity: Poland's Independent Trade Union* (Nottingham: Spokesman, 1981), Appendix 4, p. 162.

2. Dennis Vnenchak, *The Emergence and Development of the Dwarf Farm Pattern in South Poland*, doctoral dissertation, University of Massachusetts, 1990.
3. Lech Walesa, *A Way of Hope* (New York: Henry Holt, 1987), pp. 35–36.
4. Robert Eringer, *Strike for Freedom* (New York: Dodd, Mead, 1982), p. 25.
5. Quoted in Eringer, p. 24.
6. Walesa, *A Way of Hope*, pp. 41.
7. Walesa, *A Way of Hope*, pp. 49–50.
8. Walesa, *A Way of Hope*, p. 50.
9. Eringer, p. 33.
10. Walesa, *A Way of Hope*, p. 5.
11. Eringer, p. 35.
12. Eringer, p. 39.

CHAPTER FIVE

1. Author's paraphrasing of ideas expressed on April 7, 1992, in Natick, Massachusetts, by Janusz Juda, a Pole who lived through the birth of Solidarity and the declaration of martial law.
2. Quoted in Lawrence Weschler, *Solidarity: Poland in the Season of its Passion* (New York: Simon & Schuster, 1982), p. 169.
3. Timothy Garton Ash, *The Polish Revolution: Solidarity 1980–1982* (London: Jonathan Cape Ltd., 1983), p. 39.
4. Quoted in *The Book of Lech Walesa* (New York: Simon & Schuster, 1982), p. 195.
5. *The Book of Lech Walesa*, pp. 195–96.
6. Quoted in *The Book of Lech Walesa*, p. 195.
7. Adapted from Lawrence Weschler, *Solidarity: Poland in the Season of its Passion* (New York: Simon & Schuster, 1982), pp. 209–11, and Robert Eringer, *Strike for Freedom* (New York: Dodd, Mead, 1982), pp. 61–62.
8. Quoted in Eringer, p. 66.
9. Quoted in Eringer, p. 70.

CHAPTER SIX

1. Quoted in *The Book of Lech Walesa* (New York: Simon & Schuster 1982), p. 195.
2. Denis MacShane, *Solidarity: Poland's Independent Trade Union* (Nottingham: Spokesman, 1981), p. 29.

3. Neal Ascherson in *The Book of Lech Walesa* (New York: Simon & Schuster, 1982), p. 10.

4. Lech Walesa, quoted in *The Book of Lech Walesa*, pp. 198–99.

5. Quoted in MacShane, p. 162.

6. Lech Walesa told me in an interview, August 1990, that secretly he was in fact aiming for the total abolition of the Communist system in Poland, but of course, he could not admit that at the time.

7. See, for example, Alain Touraine et al., *Solidarity: Poland 1980–81* (Cambridge: Cambridge University Press, 1983).

8. Walesa in *The Book of Lech Walesa*, pp. 196–97.

CHAPTER SEVEN

1. Lech Walesa in a speech before the International Labour Conference, Geneva, June 5, 1981. Quoted in Denis MacShane, *Solidarity: Poland's Independent Trade Union* (Nottingham: Spokesman, 1981), Appendix 4, p. 162.

2. Arthur Rachwald, "The Polish Road to the Abyss," *Current History*, Nov. 1987, p. 369.

3. David S. Mason, "Stalemate and Apathy in Poland," *Current History*, Nov. 1985, p. 381.

4. Mason, p. 390.

5. David Ost, "Now Solidarity Has a Martyr," *The Nation*, March 2, 1985, pp. 237–40.

6. Mason, p. 378.

7. Lech Walesa, *A Way of Hope* (New York: Henry Holt, 1987).

8. Lech Walesa in interview with Peter Jennings for "ABC World News Tonight," Gdansk, Poland, July 10, 1989.

CHAPTER EIGHT

1. Sam Kaplan, personal communication, Boston University, April 7, 1992.

2. Robert L. Heilbroner, *The Making of Economic Society*, 8th (revised) edition (Englewood Cliffs, N.J.: Prentice-Hall, 1989), p. 91.

3. Lech Walesa, "NBC Evening News with Tom Brokaw," April 5, 1989.

4. See Richard F. Starr, "Transition in Poland," *Current History*, December 1990, p. 401.

5. See, for example, Abraham Brumberg, "Poland: The Demise of

Communism," *Foreign Affairs*, America and the World 1989–90, Vol. 69, no. 1, p. 88.

6. Starr, p. 402.

CHAPTER NINE

1. Quoted in Jule Gatter-Klenk, *Gesprache mit Lech Walesa* (Konigstein/Ts: Athenaum, 1981), back cover.
2. Lech Walesa, *A Way of Hope* (New York: Henry Holt, 1987), p. 123.
3. This interview took place in Walesa's office in the main headquarters of Solidarity in Gdansk, August 24, 1990. The interview was conducted entirely in Polish, and I took careful notes both during and immediately after the interview. I alone am completely responsible for the translation as well as its accuracy. Unless otherwise stated, all quotes by Walesa in this chapter are from this interview.
4. Michael Kort, *Nikita Khrushchev* (New York: Franklin Watts, 1989).

CHAPTER TEN

1. Neal Ascherson, *The Struggles for Poland* (New York: Random House, 1987), p. xiv.
2. Quoted in Anna Sabbat-Swidlicka, "Walesa Hails His Inauguration as Beginning of Third Republic," *Report on Eastern Europe*, vol. 2, no. 5, p. 20.
3. Quoted in David Ost, *Solidarity and the Politics of Anti-Politics* (Philadelphia: Temple University Press, 1990), p. 218.
4. Quoted in Ost, p. 214.
5. Quoted in Sabbat-Swidlicka, p. 21.
6. "Left Turn," *The Nation*, Oct. 11, 1993, p. 376.

GLOSSARY

Authoritarian rule. A type of government or leader characterized by a demand for strict obedience to authority at the expense of personal freedom and individual rights. For example, a dictatorship.

Capitalism. An economic system based on the private ownership of the means of production. Business owners make a profit by hiring laborers to produce goods that are then sold in the marketplace.

Collectivization of agriculture. The combining of small peasant farms into much larger cooperative farms, usually under state management and ownership.

Communism. According to Karl Marx, the final stage of socialism. A classless society will appear, and the state will wither away. The operating principle of society will be "from each according to his ability, to each according to his need."

Dissident. From the Latin: "one who disagrees." Often used to refer to intellectuals and political activists who radically oppose the existing system of power in a country.

Gdansk. A city on the Baltic coast of Poland, formerly known as Danzig. Home of Lech Walesa and birthplace of the Solidarity trade union.

Intelligentsia. The intellectual community or the educated class of a nation. Often used in reference to the intellectuals of East Central Europe.

Means of production. The factories, machines, tools, equipment, and land used in the production of economic goods.

Nomenklatura. The group of Communist party members, managers, and upper-level bureaucrats who dominated political and economic life in a Communist country. In Poland, depending on how it was counted, the number ranged from 200,000 to 900,000 people.

Political activist. One who is actively involved in the process of political change in a country, especially one who operates outside the traditional power center.

Political legitimacy. Political power based on the general perception by the people that the ruler or rulers have a moral or legal right to exercise control over society and enforce laws.

Political pluralism. The sharing of power among various groups or organizations in the society. In socialist Poland, this meant allowing opposition groups to coexist with the Communist party.

Regime. A government that is in power. Sometimes the word also carries a negative connotation indicating an authoritarian or dictatorial government with little or no legitimacy.

Ruling elite. A small and privileged group of people at the top of society who control most of the wealth and power.

Socialism. An economic system based on public ownership of the means of production. A socialist revolution occurs when the workers unite and rebel against the capitalists. A socialist transformation of society occurs when a country moves from capitalism to socialism.

Solidarity (Solidarność). The independent, self-governing trade union in Poland that arose out of the Gdansk strikes of August 1980 and was led by Lech Walesa.

Sovereignty. The exclusive right to rule or exercise political power. A sovereign state is independent of any other foreign state.

Strike of solidarity. A strike called by the workers of one factory in support of striking workers at another factory. Also called a sympathy strike.

Veto power. The power of an individual, social group, or political organization to block a proposed policy of the government by voicing its opposition. In Poland the threat of the workers to strike became a way for them to block government policies they did not like.

FOR FURTHER READING

Ascherson, Neal. *The Struggles for Poland.* New York: Random House, 1987.

Craig, Mary. *Lech Walesa and His Poland.* New York: Continuum, 1986.

Eringer, Robert. *Strike for Freedom! The Story of Lech Walesa and Polish Solidarity.* New York: Dodd, Mead, 1982.

Kaufman, Michael T. *Mad Dreams, Saving Graces. Poland: A Nation in Conspiracy.* New York: Random House, 1989.

MacShane, Denis. *Solidarity: Poland's Independent Trade Union.* Nottingham: Spokesman, 1981.

Michner, James A. *Poland.* New York: Random House, 1983.

Milosz, Czeslaw. *The Captive Mind.* London: Penguin, 1981.

Steven, Stewart. *The Poles.* New York: Macmillan, 1982.

Walesa, Lech. *A Way of Hope* (An Autobiography). New York: Henry Holt, 1987.

———. *The Struggle and the Triumph* (Autobiography, Part 2). New York: Arcade, 1993.

Weschler, Lawrence. *The Passion of Poland: From Solidarity through the State of War.* New York: Pantheon Books, 1984.

INDEX

INDEX

ABOUT THE AUTHOR

Dennis Vnenchak spent over six years in Poland, from 1976 to 1982, including the period when Poland was experiencing the birth of Solidarity and the imposition of martial law. After his return to the United States, he taught social science at Boston University. He is currently a visiting professor at Nicolaus Copernicus University in Torun, Poland, and a Polish representative to the TEMPUS (Ellpids) Project.